I0760144

THE BITTER FIGHT TO FREE ITALY

THE BITTER FIGHT TO FREE ITALY

A D-DAY DODGER'S EXPERIENCES OF THE ITALIAN CAMPAIGN IN 1943

DENNIS NEIL & JOHN NEIL

FRONTLINE
BOOKS

THE BITTER FIGHT TO FREE ITALY
A D-Day Dodger's Experiences of the Italian Campaign in 1943

First published in 2025 by Frontline Books, an imprint of Pen & Sword Books Ltd,
George House, Beevor Street, Barnsley, South Yorkshire, S71 1HN

ISBN: 9781036128609

 A CIP catalogue record for this book is available from the British Library.

Typeset by Lapiz Digital
Printed and bound in the UK by CPI Group (UK) Ltd,
Croydon, CR0 4YY.

Printed on paper from a sustainable source by
CPI Group (UK) Ltd, Croydon, CR0 4YY
The Publisher's authorised representative in the EU for product safety is
Authorised Rep Compliance Ltd., Ground Floor, 71 Lower Baggot Street, Dublin
D02 P593, Ireland.
www.arccompliance.com

For a complete list of Pen & Sword titles please contact:

PEN & SWORD BOOKS LTD
George House, Beevor Street, Barnsley, South Yorkshire, S71 1HN, UK.
E-mail: enquiries@pen-and-sword.co.uk
Website: www.pen-and-sword.co.uk

Or

PEN AND SWORD BOOKS,
1950 Lawrence Road, Havertown, PA 19083, USA
E-mail: Uspen-and-sword@casematepublishers.com
Website: www.penandswordbooks.com

CONTENTS

PROLOGUE

'We're the D-Day Dodgers out in Italy
Always on the vino, always on the spree.
8th Army scroungers and their tanks
We live in Rome – among the Yanks.
We are the D-Day Dodgers, over here in Italy.'

'Come on Dennis. You were one of us. Let's tell these buggers that they weren't the only ones who fought in the war!'

The song rang round the bar on the fiftieth anniversary of the D-Day landings. A public holiday and a day of national commemoration, celebrated with beer sold at 1944 prices. The location was the Merstham Football Club that served as the headquarters of the Merstham British Legion.[1] Leading the singing was Bill Lawton, the silver-haired veteran who had served as an officer in the Guards and who had fought throughout the Italian campaign.

My father did not answer, but his face was a picture of irritation. He muttered 'bloody load of rubbish' and returned to his pint.

I've often thought back on that episode. Why hadn't my father felt proud of his role in the war? Why hadn't he collected his medals and why would he never wear a poppy? It all seemed at odds with a proud man who had suffered more than most in defence of King and Country. It took me many years to unpick his story and to begin to understand the inner conflicts in a man whom his friend described as 'the bravest man I know'.

After his death, I felt I needed to know more about the Italian campaign and my father's role in it. He had told me a great deal and I was aware of his disdain for the politicians and commanders who

1 The original Merstham British Legion clubhouse that had been built by the men of Merstham after the Great War and rebuilt in 1944 after it was damaged by a flying bomb had been sold off to housing developers by the British Legion just a few years before.

had led the Allied war effort. He had also left me in no doubt that he had no time whatsoever for those who glorified war. I put this down to his lingering bitterness about his wounds and enduring pain, but his attitudes and opinions often surprised me. I bought and read many books about the war and tried to understand him better.

I was struck that many of these books focus on the military leaders and their various strategies, the moments of individual brilliance, the wins and losses and then, after each phase, the bare statistics of killed and wounded.

Almost all the British and American commanders seem to have written their memoirs, so I found no shortage of views from the top, However, other than David Vere's excellent *Give Us This Day* and Alex Bowlby's *Recollections of Rifleman Bowlby*, I found comparatively few books written by ordinary soldiers.

This book tells the story of one such soldier: my father, Dennis Neil. He was an ordinary 21-year-old private in the Royal Berkshires who, on a bitterly cold day in November 1943, was severely wounded on an Italian mountainside. This book traces his journey to that mountainside – told, as far as practical, in his own words – and how his life changed irrevocably because of the wounds he suffered that day.

John Neil

Chapter 1

MY FAMILY

I was born on 14 August 1922 at 178b Drury Lane in the West End of London. The flat in which I was born was in an ugly, drafty tenement block built in 1878. It bore the deceptively grand name of *The Bells* and stood midway down Drury Lane opposite Shorts Gardens. From the front window you could see all the way down to Seven Dials.

I was the third son of William and Nelly Neil. My father was a market porter who pulled barrows of fruit and vegetables around the market. My mother was a seed sorter, who worked separating seeds based on size, shape, and colour to ensure that only the best ones were offered for sale. She came from an English protestant family and her father, who was a fishmonger, died when she was a child. Although she did well at school she was obliged to leave at the age of 11 after Standard III.

My father had a very disrupted childhood, and little schooling. His father – my grandfather – who was also called William Neil, was born in Chatham. He was brought up by his Irish mother, Annie Harwood, and his Irish grandmother, Bridget Harwood. Bridget came from Schull, near Cork, a part of Ireland that had suffered terribly during the Great Famine of the 1840s.[2]

My grandfather had joined the Royal Navy as a 'Boy Second Class' in 1890 when he was 15 and was posted to HMS *Boscawen*, an old 70-gun ship of the line that was used as the training ship at Wellesley Nautical School in Portland. However, he soon decided that the Navy was not for him, and he absconded. When he was found he was discharged from the Navy as 'Shore Objectionable'.

2 The workhouse, which still stands in Schull, was home to around 600 inmates during this period, and the graveyard near the workhouse doubled in size during the famine years.

Following his dismissal, my grandfather travelled to London, where he found work at Covent Garden market. Shortly after his arrival, he met and fell in love with 22-year-old Honora Connor, a domestic servant who lived off Drury Lane. She was born in The Strand, but her parents came from County Kerry. I know that my grandfather loved Honora because on his right arm he wore proudly a self-inflicted tattoo: 'I L N'O'C.' The Neil family have always been romantics!

After my grandfather married Honora, they lived in a flat in Lamb's Conduit Passage. The living conditions in the streets around there were dreadful, overcrowded and unhealthy. The shops sold only second-hand items and lodgings struggled to keep up with the basic needs of their tenants. It was in these slums that my grandparents brought up seven children. As John Keats described it, 'Holborn was a place where misery clings to misery for a little warmth and want and disease lie down, side-by-side, and groan together.' (*Miller*, 1852)

My grandparents were never able to live comfortably, but they were thrown into abject misery when my grandfather was convicted for larceny in 1904 and sentenced to fifteen months in Wormwood Scrubs. With her husband in prison, Honora could no longer support herself and she was admitted to the Strand Union Workhouse in Sheffield Street, to the south of Lincoln's Inn Fields. Because my father was 11 years old, he was considered too old to enter the workhouse and so he went back to live with his Irish grandmother, Annie Harwood. This Irish matriarch was to have a lasting influence on our family.

My grandfather died shortly after his release from prison and my grandmother, my father and four of his siblings then moved to a garret flat on Ormond Yard just off Theobalds Road. To help feed the family, my father found work in Covent Garden, tending the horses of tradesmen who delivered their produce to the market.

My father began courting my mother, Nellie Kite in the summer of 1914. When she was 20 years old, she fell pregnant with my brother Bill. Although my mother and father were not married, my father was named on Bill's birth certificate and when the Great War commenced they decided to marry. Because they had a child born out of wedlock, they needed to apply for a special dispensation from the priest of the Roman Catholic church of St Anselm's and St Cecilia in the Kingsway. The dispensation was granted, subject to two conditions. Firstly, that my mother should convert to Catholicism and secondly, that Bill (and any subsequent children) should be raised as Catholics.

Shortly after their marriage, they moved into *The Bells,* which was just along the road from the 'Old Mo', the Middlesex Music Hall, which was my parents' favourite place of entertainment. Music hall provided the soundtrack to their lives and its songs of humour and cheerfulness gave them a way to laugh off their troubles. These upbeat tunes transferred to the battlefield, where my father and his comrades would sing them to keep up their spirits.

Open opposition to the war was very much marginalised in Britain and all the established organisations – political parties, trade unions, feminist organisations – supported the cause. My father answered Kitchener's call to arms voluntarily and was posted to the Army Service Corps (ASC) keeping the front-line troops supplied with provisions.

The British forces on the Western Front required a huge amount of ammunition, food and equipment. The ASC was responsible for moving this material from the Channel ports. From there, supplies were moved by train to advanced supply depots. For the final leg, they were moved by horse, mule or motor transport to the quartermaster staff of front-line units. Unlike carts and other wheeled vehicles, horses and other pack animals could travel almost anywhere a soldier could go on foot, including roads that had been destroyed by shelling or were swamped with mud. Teams of horses were also used to pull the 18-pounder artillery guns and for pulling ambulances to transport injured soldiers from casualty clearing stations to field hospitals.

Because of my father's experience with horses, he was soon transferred to the Army Veterinary Corps (AVC) treating sick and wounded horses, donkeys and mules on the battlefields of France and Belgium. The use of gas, artillery, mines, machine guns, mortars and tanks made the front line a terrifying place for horses. In the early days of gas warfare, nose plugs and horse gas masks were developed. Thousands of horses were caught up in barbed wire and suffered injuries as they struggled to escape. Leg wounds suffered by horses often failed to heal or became infected, and the animals would have to be shot. My father and the other men of the AVC performed wonders in patching up injured and wounded horses and War Office records show that 2½ million horses were treated in AVC veterinary hospitals, with 2 million restored to sufficiently good health that they could be returned to service.

When the Armistice was signed on 11 November 1918, my mother joined the crowds gathered in Trafalgar Square to celebrate. However, the joyful mood was short-lived. So many men had perished in the war or had suffered life-affecting wounds; for them and their families life would never be the same.

My father emerged unscathed from the war, but like many other servicemen he was retained in France with rumours growing that men were about to be posted to Russia. After the Armistice the men were told that they were needed to rescue the British and French soldiers that had become trapped in Russia after the 1917 October Revolution. Then, the message changed. They were now needed to help the White Russian forces in the Russian Civil War. This was a quite different proposition and was very unpopular with men who were war weary and whose natural sympathies were with the revolutionaries rather than the White Russians.

As the delays to demobilisation became prolonged, unrest grew. The French army descended into open mutiny and the British soldiers proved that they were equally unwilling to obey orders from military leaders for whom they had lost all respect. This caused alarm among the Army command and a mutiny by soldiers at Étaples in September 1918 led to five youths aged 17 to 19 being sentenced to ten years' imprisonment. These savage sentences did nothing to cool the temperature.

The mood in the camp at Étaples where my father was held was particularly bad, while just up the road, the men of the Army Ordnance and Mechanical Transport sections at the Valdelièvre camp[3] voted to mutiny. This decision was taken after the arrest of Private John Pantling, of the Army Ordnance Corps, for delivering what was described as a 'seditious speech' (Parker, 2009). On pay day the men at Valdelièvre broke into the prison block in an unsuccessful attempt to get Pantling out.

The newly organised Soldiers' Councils then called a strike and the next morning not a single man turned up for reveille. Later that same day, at another camp in nearby Vendreux, more than 2,000 men came out in sympathy and marched to the Calais camp as a gesture of solidarity. After a mass meeting, both camps marched behind brass bands towards the British Army headquarters at Montreuil-sur-Mer.

Having surrounded the headquarters, a deputation entered the building demanding the release of Private Pantling. By now some 20,000 men – of whom my father was one – had joined the mutiny and the strike was spreading with French workers placing a total embargo upon the movement of British military traffic by rail. The rail stoppage prevented 5,000 infantrymen from returning home, so they also joined the strike. To intimidate the mutineers, General Julian 'Bungo' Byng called in fresh troops, but Byng made the mistake of arriving before

3 Valdelièvre is not a place. It is the name of the owners of a former timberyard in Calais that had been used as a camp by the Army.

the men and his car was commandeered by the mutineers. Byng's reinforcements then joined the strikers.

The mutiny at Calais led to a wave of mutinies all over the south-east of England, including at several London railway stations where troops refused to embark for Russia and France. On 3 January 1919, most of the garrison at Folkestone refused to attend reveille in protest at poor food, excessive officer privileges and orders that they return to France. The *Daily Herald* on 11 January described the event:

> On their own signal – three taps of a drum – two thousand men, unarmed and in perfect order, demonstrated the fact that they were fed up – absolutely fed up. Their plan of action had been agreed upon the night before: no military boat should be allowed to leave Folkestone for France that day or any day until they were guaranteed their freedom ... On Saturday a great procession of soldiers, swelled now to about 10,000 marched through the town. Everywhere the townspeople showed their sympathy. (*Daily Herald*, 1919)

Similar soldiers' protests, strikes, riots and mutinies took place in cities, ports and barracks all over Britain. These incidents shook the authorities. British troops had shown they could organise and forge links with the civilian population. Faced with the threat of a full-scale rebellion, army chiefs hastily agreed to improve conditions in the camps and speed up demobilisation, fearing that a revolution was brewing.

When the strike was eventually called off, the authorities never felt strong enough to victimise the strike committees or to reimpose the old style of military discipline. It was agreed that soldiers were free to return to camp whenever they felt like it, and to enter cafes during 'prohibited' hours, without fear of disciplinary action. The food they were given was improved, new billet huts were erected, and weekend work was abolished.

Within three months demobilisation began in earnest, only just in time to avert another wave of mutiny. As Churchill commented astutely: 'If these armies had formed a united resolve, if they had been seduced from the standards of duty and patriotism, there was no power which could have attempted to withstand them.' (Churchill, *The World Crisis*, 1929)

However, the fact is most of the men were not looking to start a revolution, they simply wanted to go home to their families.

When my father came home, he found a pall of grief hanging over the Covent Garden community. Wives had lost their husbands and sons; sweethearts had lost their fiancés; and there were gaps in the management and workforce of every company. As the injured, gassed, shell-shocked, blinded men came back, those who were too young to fight vowed 'never again', determined to live life to the full. Fashions changed dramatically and so did standards of morality. New scientific inventions and experiments in art, music and literature reflected a determination to move on from the past. A new day had dawned.

My father was not needed in his old job but he found work as a market porter on piece-rate. The job paid well in the busy summer months when produce was plentiful but work and the rate of pay declined significantly in the winter months. Those who had fought in the war and who had become more aware of their power, began to flex their muscles. The Government and the right-wing press went into panic as the police and railway workers called strikes and a shortage of apples led to criminality that the *Daily Telegraph* branded as 'terrorism'.

The notion that men who had volunteered to fight in the war were in some way unpatriotic because they were now demanding a living wage was deeply disrespectful to the strikers. Labour politicians pointed out the paradox that although war had impoverished Britain and had severely depleted its gold and currency reserves, some people had done very well out of the misery and now was the time for that wealth to be shared.

Resentment about the gap between rich and poor was reinforced among the large Anglo-Irish community in Covent Garden by a growing sense of grievance about the attitude of the British government to the Irish War of Independence. Winston Churchill, who was then the Secretary of State for War, was already an unpopular figure after Gallipoli and the attempted intervention in the Russian Civil War. The imprisonment of seventy-three members of Sinn Fein following Churchill's allegation that they had participated in a 'German plot' and his enthusiastic endorsement of the proposal to send ex-servicemen to crush dissent in Ireland made him a hated figure.

The head of the Royal Irish Constabulary (RIC), General Joseph Byrne objected to Churchill's proposal to send troops to Ireland on the grounds that ex-soldiers could not be controlled by police discipline. He was soon replaced by General Sir Nevil Macready, a career British Army officer with a reputation for being a tough, unsentimental, Unionist sympathiser. In December 1919, advertisements were placed in British newspapers calling for men willing to 'face a rough and dangerous task'. (*Scoular*, 2015).

About 10,000 ex-servicemen came forward and this led to the Irish president, Éamonn de Valera, denouncing the RIC as agents of the 'foreign usurper' whose 'history [was] a continuity of brutal treason against their own people'. (*Scoular, 2015*)

The new RIC recruits were issued with a mixture of dark tunics and caps, and khaki army trousers. These uniforms differentiated them from both the regular RIC and the British Army and gave rise to their nickname: Black and Tans. The commanding officer of the Black and Tans was Lieutenant Colonel Gerald Smyth, a Unionist sympathiser who had lost an arm in the Great War, and he told the new recruits:

> Should the order 'Hands Up' not be immediately obeyed, shoot and shoot with effect. If the persons approaching a patrol carry their hands in their pockets, or are in any way suspicious looking, shoot them down. You may make mistakes occasionally and innocent persons may be shot, but that cannot be helped, and you are bound to get the right parties some time. The more you shoot, the better I will like you, and I assure you no policeman will get into trouble for shooting any man … hunger-strikers will be allowed to die in jail, the more the merrier. Some of them have died already and a damn bad job they were not all allowed to die. Any man who is prepared to be a hindrance rather than a help to us, had better leave the job at once. (*Irish Bulletin*, 9 July 1920)

The speech caused outrage among the Irish and Anglo-Irish communities and made Smyth a marked man. On the evening of 17 July 1920, he was in the smoking room of the Cork and County Club when a six-man IRA team led by Dan 'Sandow' O'Donovan entered and told him: 'Colonel, were not your orders to shoot on sight? Well, you are in sight now, so prepare.' (*Hart, 1998*) Colonel Smyth jumped to his feet before being shot in the head, chest and heart.

The Black and Tans responded by conducting a series of arbitrary reprisals. These included the burning of homes, businesses, meeting halls and farms. Buildings were attacked with gunfire and grenades, and businesses were looted. In early November, Black and Tans besieged Tralee in revenge for the IRA abduction and killing of two local RIC men. They closed all the businesses in the town, let no food in for a week and shot dead three local civilians. Stories of these atrocities filled the British papers. This account from the *Nottingham and Midland Catholic News* dated Saturday, 4 June 1921 is particularly graphic:

> Last Christmas a party of Black and Tans looted a public-house in Ardfert, Co. Kerry, and what liquor they were unable to consume they heaved into the lorry. On the return journey they espied a barefooted little girl of fifteen crossing a bog. One of the 'police' bet a comrade of his,

> a bottle of whiskey that he would not 'get her.' He took aim and killed the girl. Her name was Connell.
>
> In another portion of the same county, a short time ago, a lorry-load of Crown forces came upon four young men who had been attending a mission, sitting on a wall, as is the way with young men in Ireland, after the day's work. One of these made his escape with only some superficial bullet-wounds. The 'police' took the other three into a field, and having broken every bone in their bodies, riddled them with bullets. (*Nottingham and Midland Catholic News*, 1921)

These reports were read avidly in Covent Garden and led many members of the Anglo-Irish community to align themselves with the Irish rebels and there was much celebration when Churchill lost his seat in the House of Commons to Edwin Scrymgeour.[4] Britain was still a long way from a revolution, but unrest was growing.

---

4 During the election campaign Scrymgeour had said that it would not surprise him in the event of civil war in Britain if Churchill were at the head of the Fascisti party. (Wrigley, 2006)

Chapter 2

MY CHILDHOOD

So, this was the troubled backdrop to my childhood. I had four siblings: Bill, Jimmy, Nora and Jeremiah (Bert).[5] We were all given traditional family names, so I was never quite sure how my mother and father came up with the name 'Jeremiah'. My mother used to tease me: 'He's Jeremiah, but you're just plain Dennis.'

All the Neil children were born with the assistance of female midwives and matrons from the Lying-in Hospital in Endell Street. Prior to the hospital's creation, childbirth was a domestic affair relying on untrained (but well-experienced) midwives as only the rich were served by doctors. For women like my mother, the British Lying-In Hospital was a blessing, providing a female-only space away from my father!

My parents always lived close to the breadline, but when I was just 2 years old, they were impoverished by the Covent Garden strike. The strike was called in response to a proposal by the Covent Garden employers to reduce porterage rates. The representatives of the employers claimed that the new piece-rates would enable the porters to earn £12 per week in the summer and £3 to £5 in the winter, but these rates depended on the porters being employed full-time. The casual system almost guaranteed that porters would never be employed year-round and that they would often have periods of unemployment where they would earn nothing at all. As the *Daily Herald* reported, when a representative of the employers announced the new rates and their terms he was greeted by 'hisses and boos' from the porters.

Ben Tillett, a prominent trade unionist and a Member of Parliament, played a crucial role in supporting the strikers. Tillett addressed mass

5 My mother also had two other girls after Bert, named Mary and Eileen, but they both died as infants.

meetings of the Covent Garden porters, offering them encouragement and rallying public support for their cause. His involvement brought greater attention to the strike, highlighting the broader issues of labour rights and fair treatment for workers.

The aim of the strikers was to stifle the supply of fruit and vegetables to London restaurants and hotels. However, they were outflanked by the growers and retailers who supplied their own blacklegs, who worked under police protection. The Labour Government implored the Covent Garden employers to negotiate with the union, but they refused on the grounds that the strike was 'inspired by communist revolutionaries'.

The *Daily Telegraph* elaborated on this theme:

> This strike illustrates very effectively the manner in which the public is suffering from the unrestricted action of the trade union leaders who are concerned with what are known as sheltered industries. The strike of the Covent Garden porters will not prove an unmixed curse if it serves once more to direct attention to the injustice which the high wages of such unskilled men, with their close trade unionism, represent to others, who have to be satisfied with what their labour will fetch in a world market. (*The Covent Garden Strike, 1920*)

Without pay, the market porters and their families were soon living hand to mouth, depending on help from friends, neighbours and sympathetic shopkeepers for food to eat. In the early 1970s my mother's best friend, Nell Johnson, was interviewed for the London Weekend Television programme *Aquarius* and she told a story about how, in the middle of the strike, she had managed to get hold of some kippers from a kindly fishmonger. She had placed the fish on her plate in her kitchen, but because it was a sweltering day she had left the window open. In crept a very hungry cat who snaffled the kippers. When Nell's husband came home, he was furious and threw the cat out the window!

As the days passed with no sign of a resolution of the strike, the union leaders called on the dockers to stop the cross-Channel service for fruit and vegetables, but this was not enough to halt trade and with many families facing starvation the strike was called off on 24 September 1924. The decision was greeted with relief and barely suppressed jubilation in the right-wing press:

> Mr Bevin has had to admit that his attempt to hold up Covent Garden and the food of the nation has failed. This foolish strike may well be a

> lesson to the workers not to blindly follow the advice of leaders whose sole aim seems to be to cause the greatest amount of annoyance and inconvenience to the public. The porters at Covent Garden had no real grievance. They have willingly gone back to work on the old conditions. Every credit is due to the employers for the firm attitude they adopted from the beginning. They fought a just cause and were never in doubt to the ultimate result. They have supplied the public with their goods without much trouble, and today the men are back at work without any trace of animosity. The attempts to bring out railwaymen and transport workers failed miserably. It is a tribute to these Unions that they will not down tools unless they are convinced of the justice of the cause. (*The Covent Garden Strike, 1924*)

Among the porters of Covent Garden, the attitude of the employers compounded their sense of injustice and deep distrust of capitalism and the British state.

However, for all this, Covent Garden market was still a happy place where a large community in a similar predicament lived, worked, played and drank together. Although Anglo-Irish families predominated, many of our neighbours were Italians – the Minaris, the Campanas and the Pattarinis – and it was no great surprise when my brother Bill started courting, and later married, an Italian girl, Anna 'Netta' Quattromini from 'Little Italy' off the Theobalds Road.

Before the war, Gus Elen, the coster comedian, sang a cockney dialect comic song with the title: *'E Don't Know Where 'E Are'*, which mocked those who had aspirations above their station. However, my parents preferred the 'answer' song 'I'm *the Man Who Don't Know Where 'E Are'*, in which the singer celebrates coming into money and has no reservations about showing off:

> No more down to Covent Garden
> Lugging sack of 'tatters on me back
> No more cord-er-roy or hob-nailed boots
> I'm so well dressing now.
>
> I've thrown out all my coster hats.
> And chucked away the end of my cigar.
> When I go out a-walking, the gels they all declare
> 'Here comes the man who don't know where 'e are.'

They may have had little spare money but the Neil children were always properly fed and well dressed, and my mother and father always seemed to have enough for a pint or two of Guinness!

An annual event that attracted much public attention in the market was the competition to find the porter who could carry the most boxes on his head. My father was no match for porter Jim Sainsbury, who featured in a Pathé newsreel, billed as 'the Covent Garden Cinquevalli'. He could carry twenty baskets over the course without dropping a single one.

When I was 5 years old, I started attending Macklin Street Roman Catholic School, where I was educated by nuns (or 'Holy Sisters' as we called them). Just a few years before I started there, the Holy Sisters had petitioned the Home Secretary to show mercy to two IRA men, Reginald Dunne and Joseph O'Sullivan, who were former pupils of the school. They had been sentenced to death for the assassination of Field Marshal Sir Henry Wilson, the Military Advisor to the Ulster Government. He was the man perceived to be responsible for the murder of Catholics in the North and for pronouncements advocating the reinvasion of the South.

The plot had been hatched on the evening of 21 June 1922 at an IRA meeting at Mooney's in The Strand. The meeting, which had been called to discuss the split caused by the Anglo-Irish Treaty, took an unexpected turn when reference was made to an article in the *Pall Mall Gazette* that announced Field Marshal Sir Henry Wilson MP would be unveiling a war memorial in the main booking hall of Liverpool Street Station on the following day.

Michael Collins, in his position as president of the Irish Republican Brotherhood (IRB), called for volunteers to assassinate Wilson and Dunne and O'Sullivan stepped forward. Both men had served and been wounded with the British Army during the war. Dunne walked with a permanent limp and O'Sullivan had lost a leg at the Battle of Passchendaele.

The two men lay in wait for Wilson outside his home at 36 Eaton Place and shot him dead on his own doorstep after he returned from the unveiling of the memorial. The shooting enraged the British government, who resolved to suppress the unrest in Ireland. David Lloyd George sent an ultimatum to Michael Collins and the provisional Irish government that evening stating that if they did not remove the anti-Treaty garrison from Ireland's main courts building, the 'Four Courts', the British would do it for them. Six days later, the provisional government shelled the building, so beginning the Irish Civil War.

Dunne and O'Sullivan were arrested shortly after the shooting and placed on trial for murder. Their appeal for clemency was rejected and both men were executed at Wandsworth Prison. O'Sullivan's last letter to his father, which was published in the *Daily Herald*, contained the lines: 'Although I die in the eyes of this country a felon, remember the felon's cap is the noblest crown an Irish head can wear.' (*Daily Herald*, 1922)

The story of Dunne and O'Sullivan's sacrifice – but not their crime – was told to us repeatedly by the Holy Sisters, who ensured that we remembered that Ireland could never be free until it was rid of the British occupiers.[6]

Overall, Macklin Street was a fine school, and I enjoyed my time there and all my studies. I also represented the school at football, swimming at the Oasis Open Air Baths and in the Westminster Schools Athletic Association annual boxing championships at Watney's Gymnasium in Victoria.

I was encouraged to box by my father, who was well-known around Covent Garden market for his boxing skills. In August 1928, when I was just 6 years old, he took me to the Ring at Blackfriars to see Jack Hood fight Len Johnson. The match had taken on a particular significance in the eyes of the British press because Hood was white British, while Len Johnson was black and reputed to be a member of the Communist Party.

Although Britain was still – for the most part – a tolerant society, the black population of Britain had grown during the Great War, and the right-wing press had stirred up trouble by suggesting that Britain was under threat as a strong, homogenous and essentially white nation because of foreign (i.e., black and Asian) invaders.

There were 3,000 people in the Ring that night with a further 10,000 outside and the atmosphere was electric. After the match, my father introduced me to Jimmy Wilde, who had held the World Flyweight championship from 1916 to 1923. I had never felt more in awe of my father that he knew such men.

I remember another occasion when my father demonstrated his boxing ability on the street outside our flat. A man – a stranger – had just emerged, very much worse for wear, from the Sun public house on the corner of Betterton Street and Drury Lane. In front of a group of women, he started to perform a striptease, taking off one item of clothing as he sang each verse of this song:

6 There is a fascinating article about the role of Holy Sisters in promoting Irish independence in an article entitled 'It was the Presentation nuns who made a rebel of me' on the Taylor & Francis Online website.

This old hat that I've got on, the crown of it is gone,
The brim it is all come asunder.
If I only had one more, if I only had a score,
I would keep this old hat to remember.

This old boot that I've got on, the sole of it is gone,
The tongue it is all come asunder ...
This old coat that I've got on, the sleeve of it is gone,
The pockets are all come asunder ...

This old shirt that I've got on, the tail of it is gone,
The collar is all come asunder ...
These old breeches I've got on, the crutch of it is gone,
The arse it is all come asunder.

Unamused, my father shouted out of the window for him to pack it in. When the man responded with a volley of abuse, my father leapt down the stairs and squared up to him in the street in Drury Lane. The man threw a punch with his right fist, which my father dodged neatly. Before the man could throw another punch, my father knocked him out cold with a straight left jab. He told me that night: 'Son, I knew he was a mug when he led with his right.' That was a boxing lesson I never forgot!

The cramped, cold and drafty condition of our flat was not compatible with marital bliss and my siblings and I got very used to seeing our parents drunk and at each other's throats, rowing about the most trivial of issues. I remember one argument over who sang 'Waiting at the Church': Vesta Victoria or Kate Carney?[7] It sounds comical now, but it wasn't very funny at the time.

When I was about 10 or 11, I became an altar boy at Corpus Christi Catholic Church in Maiden Lane. The Church was known as the 'Actors' Church' and was the home to the Catholic Stage Guild,[8] who offered spiritual support to Catholic actors and actresses working in the West End. I'm told that the novelist Radclyffe Hall and her partner Lady Una Troubridge worshipped there for a time in the 1920s, but I can't say that I ever noticed them.[9]

---

7 Nellie and her friends used to drink in the Crossed Keys in Endell Street, while Bill used various pubs around the market.

8 The Guild was created to 'encourage spiritual, artistic and social intercourse among Catholics connected with the theatrical and allied professions'.

9 The church is also mentioned in Graham Greene's novel *The End of the Affair*.

It was here that I soaked up further stories from Irish history and tales of British perfidy. I was told that my real name was 'O'Neil', not 'Neil' and that I should be proud of my bloodline to Red Hugh O'Neil, who had led the Irish clans against the English King. When I was confirmed, I was given the third name 'Patrick'.

Around this time, I won a LCC scholarship that enabled me to go to Salesian College in Battersea. This was a Catholic fee-paying college for boys aged 11 to 18. The teachers at the College were Catholic Brothers, some of whom had developed a keen taste for sadism. Beatings of small boys were commonplace for the smallest of misdemeanours.

Most of the Catholic Brothers were not particularly political, but there was one who seemed bent on inspiring a revolution. I remember a lesson where he read, with great enthusiasm, an appeal that was made by the Irish Republican Army (IRA) to the Orangemen:

> Capitalism and imperialism constitute a system of exploitation and injustice – within which the mass of the people can know no freedom. We can see no permanent solution of these evils except the transfer of power over production, distribution and exchange to the mass of the people. The freedom of the mass of the Irish people is impossible without breaking the connection with Imperial Britain and with all the Imperial system connotes. You surely must see that your future is bound with the mass of the people in the remainder of Ireland. (*Londonderry Sentinel*, 1932)

However, the Brothers' rhetoric and urgings passed over our heads. I think we were more interested in football!

I was regularly mocked by some of the older boys for my Drury Lane accent, but I can't say it bothered me much. I am naturally resilient, and I was never bullied. I made it into the College football team, playing at right half, but my assertive playing style did not make me universally popular. In one keenly contested match I launched a sliding tackle that sent one of the opposing team crashing into the goalpost. One of the other boys remarked: 'Oh Neil, I didn't think even you could sink that low.' I had never felt so guilty or so misunderstood. I didn't mean to hurt him; I only wanted to stop him scoring.

Chapter 3

HOP-PICKING

Holidays – such as they were – were spent hop picking. We normally went between 4 and 15 September, when we were supposed to be back at school. Hop picking not only provided the money to tide our family over the winter, but was also an opportunity for us children to take in much-needed country air.

Several of the Covent Garden families went to Old Place Farm in Sandhurst every year. Come March, the cry would go up 'Have you got your letter yet?' as William Reeves, the farmer started to write to families confirming that they were welcome to pick hops at his farm again.

When the big day arrived, my mother would pack up all our belongings into a 'hopping box' that contained everything we required: candles, lamps, pots, water jugs, kitchen utensils, etc for our stay in a hut on the farm. Starting out around midnight, we used to walk all the way to London Bridge Station to catch the 'Hoppers' Specials'. (My father and the other men had to stay at home to work, as there was no paid leave in those days.)

The train that carried us wound its way through the night, stopping at virtually every station along the line. I had to be woken up to change trains at Paddock Wood and Tonbridge, and in total the 35-mile journey took over six hours.

Travelling at night meant that the trains were cheap, but we were packed in so tight that we had to sit on the floor of the carriage with the little ones in the luggage racks. To save the cost of some of the fares, some of the other children were smuggled through the ticket barrier under their mothers' dresses. My mother never tried that!

Once we arrived at Bodiam station, Reeves would be waiting with his cart ready to transport our luggage and the elderly and infirm up to the farm. The fit and able had to walk behind the cart a couple of miles up Bodiam hill to Sandhurst.

By the mid-1930s we gave up the inconvenience of the train and travelled down to Sandhurst on a lorry borrowed from one of the farmers who supplied the market. My mother and the other women would sit on dining chairs on the flat bed of the lorry while Nora, Bertie and I sat on the floor. The lorry enabled us to take more belongings from home including tables, chairs, rugs, curtains, and real beds. My mother used to put up flowery wallpaper to make the hut look more homely. One year we even acquired the luxury of a single-ring paraffin stove to boil a kettle.

When we travelled by lorry we used to stop regularly at pubs along the way, starting with the Crossed Keys in Endell Street, no more than 100 yards away from our flat. It always seemed to me that it took even longer to get there by lorry than it did when we went by train!

I can remember clearly that even though my mother was always very happy – elated even – to be going hopping, she and the other mothers were always particularly anxious when they travelled over Hartlake Bridge in Golden Green. The bridge spans the River Medway about a mile east of Sevenoaks and my mother called it the 'Devil's Punchbowl'. The cause of their anxiety was a folk memory passed down through the generations of a tragedy that occurred there on the evening of 20 October 1853. A wagon had been taking forty hop pickers and their families back to their campsite from the hop gardens where they had been working. One of the horses pulling the wagon shied, causing its wheels to crash through the side of the bridge. This upended the cart, tipping its passengers into the river, which was swollen in flood. The forty victims, who were aged between 2 and 59 years old, were all either Irish or Romany from one extended family.[10]

At the inquest, the coroner found that the accident arose entirely from the defective state of the wooden bridge, which should have been fixed by the Medway Navigation Company. The coroner's condemnation was barely acknowledged by the Company, who refused to accept any liability or to contribute to the cost of the funerals and these had to be borne by the parishioners of Hadlow. Perhaps, unsurprisingly,

---

10 A monument in the form of an oast house has been erected in the grounds of St Mary's Church, Hadlow. The monument is Grade II listed. There is one omission from the names of those who died and that is that of the youngest victim, a 2-year-old girl whose parents died with her in the accident.

whenever my mother crossed a bridge all you could hear was the rattling of rosary beads![11]

The hoppers' hut that we stayed in was about 3 metres square, made of brick and had a corrugated tin roof. Our hut had a small window, but others had no windows with the only light coming in through the doors that were left open all day. In the winter the farmers sometimes used our hut as a shelter for sheep. Modest though these huts were, at least they provided us with a degree of privacy, which was a significant improvement on our grandparents' day when the hoppers were all housed in communal barns.

Reeves, the farmer, provided us with a cookhouse, which had a fireplace with a bar across it to hang cooking pots. Each family of hop pickers was entitled to several faggots, which were bundles of small tree branches that were tied together and used for the fires. To protect the faggots until they were required, they were used to form a base for our beds. To make a mattress, two sheets were sown together and stuffed with straw. The beds were extremely uncomfortable because the straw would stick through the sheets until it was flattened down. I'll never forget the earwigs, which seemed to be everywhere.

Water was provided through communal taps, which were located close to the road, but the sanitary conditions in the huts were very basic. Toilets were small sheds with a plank of wood that went over a hole in the ground. We had to throw lime down the hole to fend off the smell.

Several Romany families took part in the hop picking at Sandhurst, staying in their caravans (or 'vardo' as they called them) at the far-right side of the common. One Romany family, the Lees, used to set their vardo in the orchard right at the back of our hut.

My mother and the other mothers started work in the hop gardens at 7 a.m. every morning (except Sundays), which meant that they had to make an early start getting our food and drink ready for the day. They stopped for breakfast and a dinner break but otherwise worked through until 6 p.m. in the evening, while we mostly played around all day among the hop bines.

---

11 A near repeat of the Hartlake Bridge tragedy occurred after the war on Friday, 12 September 1947 at Bodiam. For some reason that has never been fully explained, a lorry carrying around thirty hop pickers from the Guinness hop garden crashed through temporary railings at the side of Bodiam bridge, falling 10ft into the river below. One of the survivors commented: 'If it hadn't been for the actions of several German PoWs who joined in the rescue there would certainly have been deaths. The prisoners did not receive any recognition for their deeds and were never named.'

At the end of the harvest, all the pickers were paid out according to the number of bushels they had picked, but our final pay packet was usually quite small because Farmer Reeves was quite happy to pay out a proportion of our earnings mid-week to enable us children to go to the local shop for fresh provisions and sweets, and to the *The Harrier* the local pub to pick up a bottle of Guinness or two for my mother, and to collect the deposits from her empties.

Weekends were the most exciting times, as this is when my father and the other men came down to visit us. They were not allowed to drink in the *The Harrier* or any of the other local pubs in Sandhurst village, who put out 'home dwellers only' signs. My mother and father and all the other Drury Lane hop-pickers used to walk down the hill to the *The White Hart* at Newenden or the *The Castle Inn* at Bodiam. In these two pubs, the hop pickers were always welcome, with drinks being served through a hatch (with a deposit of a shilling or tanner to ensure the glasses were returned).

In 1933, dad took my sister, Nora and my younger brother, Bertie and me to Hastings and challenged me to swim round the Rock-a-Nore groyne that provides a harbour for the Hastings fishing fleet. To my immense pride, I did it easily and he gave me a shilling as a reward.

Although these hop-picking holidays were incredibly happy, carefree times for our family, the effects of poverty were never far away. In 1929, the 10-year-old daughter of one of the Drury Lane hop pickers caught smallpox and died there on the very day that she arrived in Sandhurst. She was buried at the front of the churchyard of St Nicholas' Church under a simple wooden cross. I went back there in 1974, and the cross was still standing, but it has long since rotted and been cleared away in a tidying up exercise, leaving no trace of this small tragedy almost a century ago.

Chapter 4

OUTBREAK OF WAR

When I left Salesian College in 1938, my father found me my first job as an office clerk in a Covent Garden market sales office. My brothers, Billy and Jimmy, were already working there as market porters while my younger brother, Bert was working as a lift attendant in a West End department store and my sister Nora was working as a factory hand. We were all still living at home at *The Bells*.

As a teenager, I loved to read books of all kinds. My favourite author was Ernest Hemingway, and I admired his story telling and his economic, under-stated style. I also read widely about American and Irish history. Although I considered myself a socialist, none of the political parties held any appeal. Democracy seemed to me to be nothing more than a means of maintaining the status quo. In fact, world affairs rarely troubled me at all, and I was largely unaware of the sparks that were to ignite the Second World War.

However, when I was 17, the Secretary of State for War, Leslie Hore-Belisha, persuaded the cabinet of Neville Chamberlain to introduce a limited form of conscription for all single men aged between 20 and 22.[12] My brothers Bill and Jimmy were both caught up by this. Billy joined the Army and Jimmy joined the Navy.

On 3 September 1939, we all listened in silence to Neville Chamberlain's radio broadcast in which he announced the declaration of war against Germany. Shortly after that, the National Service (Armed Forces) Act 1939 came into force, which lowered the age of conscription for men to 18. Although I was still too young to be affected, I listened to Churchill's words with trepidation:

12 The intention was for the first intake to undergo six months of basic training before being discharged into an active reserve. They would then be recalled for short training periods at an annual camp.

> There is a generation of Britons here now ready to prove itself not unworthy of the days of yore and not unworthy of those great men, the fathers of our land, who laid the foundations of our laws and shaped the greatness of our country. This is not a question of fighting for Danzig or fighting for Poland. We are fighting to save the whole world from the pestilence of Nazi tyranny and in defence of all that is most sacred to man. (*Sunderland Daily Echo and Shipping Gazette*, 1939)

My nervousness turned into outright anxiety when the Germans invaded the Low Countries in May 1940. In the space of just twenty-four days, Belgium and Holland were overrun and the German army reached the Channel coast. The 330,000 British and French troops who were evacuated from Dunkirk reached Britain bedraggled and without most of their weapons and equipment, leaving many thousands in France killed, missing or as prisoners of war. We all knew then just how serious the position had become.

Shortly after Dunkirk, Chamberlain went to Buckingham Palace to resign and advise the King to send for Winston Churchill, who became Britain's Prime Minister on 10 May 1940. As Churchill was to write: 'I felt … that all my past life had been but a preparation for this hour and for this trial.' (*Morin*, 1965) I can't say the appointment thrilled me; he was still a villain in my eyes.

By the middle of June, France had surrendered, and Britain had an army wholly inadequate for the task of defending her shores from an invasion that seemed imminent. I realised that it was only a matter of time before I would be called up to do my bit.

Chapter 5

AFTER DUNKIRK

After Dunkirk, Britain had nowhere to turn but to America, but America was not ready to come to help Britain. In the USA, the Neutrality Acts of 1935 and 1937 had been introduced to prevent the economic ties that had helped drag America into the Great War. These acts prevented the sale of arms to foreign powers and mandated that all goods purchased by foreign governments had to be collected by the buyer and paid for at the time of purchase.

President Franklin D. Roosevelt was a keen supporter of America's neutrality. He insisted: 'I have seen war. I hate war.' Three thousand miles of Atlantic Ocean must have seemed like adequate protection against Hitler's Germany, while the expansion of Italy or Japan was of limited concern to a country with few overseas possessions and little dependence on foreign trade. Britain could not afford to take such a detached view. Britain's interests lay not just in preventing war but also in protecting the vulnerable trade routes on which the British Empire depended. British politicians wanted peace, but not at any price.

Churchill pleaded with Roosevelt for the loan of some American destroyers that were laid up in dockyards on the US East Coast after the Great War. Churchill argued that these ships could be used to protect the Atlantic sea lanes. Roosevelt's reply was one that Churchill would become used to receiving: he wanted to help, but Congress would not allow it. Churchill replied: 'We must ask … as a matter of life or death to be reinforced with these destroyers.' (*Devine,* 1966)

Roosevelt did not reply and for two months after the fall of France he sent no messages at all because he was preoccupied with the American presidential election. He told a husting meeting in Brooklyn:

> I am only fighting for a free America – for a country in which all men and women have equal rights to liberty and justice … I'm fighting to keep

> this nation prosperous and at peace. I'm fighting to keep our people out of foreign wars, and to keep foreign conceptions of government out of our own United States. (*Roosevelt*, 1944)

In desperation, Churchill cabled on 31 July 1940: 'Mr President, with great respect I must tell you that in the long history of the world, this is a thing to do now.' (*Renwick*, 1996)

As the US election campaign ended, the Republican challenger, Wendell Willkie, warned that Roosevelt's re-election would lead to the deployment of American soldiers abroad. In response, Roosevelt promised that: 'Your boys are not going to be sent into any foreign wars.' (*Gillon*, 2011)

Roosevelt duly won the 1940 election with 55 per cent of the popular vote, but even after he was secure in office, he was unwilling to abandon his policy of neutrality. There was a widespread belief in Washington that Britain was on the verge of collapse and Roosevelt estimated Britain's chances of survival as no better than one in three.

Roosevelt did agree to sell rifles to Britain (and France) to enable the newly formed Local Defence Volunteers (Home Guard) to be armed, but this was still a commercial arrangement with strings attached. America would sell the arms provided Britain and France paid in US dollars (or gold) and sent ships to collect them: a so-called 'cash and carry' arrangement.

The joint contract was for 600,000 rifles, 25,000 light machine guns, 20,000 medium machine guns and large stocks of ammunition. The US rifles had all been manufactured in 1917–18 and had been packed away in grease for more than twenty years. The price demanded was an eye-watering $37 million ($643 million at today's value).

In February 1939, France had purchased 100 Douglas DB-7 light bombers from the USA. At this time, France was not considered a belligerent nation, and the sale did not violate the existing Neutrality Acts. In early 1940, Paul Reynaud, the French prime minister, tried to buy more American military aircraft, but the reality was that in June 1940 America had few spare aircraft to sell. On 16 June Reynaud resigned and was replaced by Phillipe Pétain, who asked Germany for an armistice. Some of the Douglas aircraft supplied previously by America were moved to Martinique in the French West Indies, where they remained until 1944.

The fall of France presented Britain with another emergency in addition to the threat of invasion. On 15 June 1940, the day after German troops marched down the Champs Elysees, Arthur Purvis, the US-based head of the British Purchasing Commission, received a telegram from London warning that the surrender of France might come at any moment. If France should sue for peace, Britain would be left to face Germany alone, with all joint contracts subject to legal disputes. French orders for arms worth over $500 million might be terminated.

Many of the contracts were for supplies the British would need if they were to carry on fighting. Other contracts were for special French equipment and would be worthless to Britain. There were literally thousands of contracts; it would take weeks to examine them, pick out what the British needed, and then negotiate with the manufacturers on an individual basis. There would not be time. Purvis decided there and then that the British must take on all the French contracts.

In Purvis's apartment in New York, they went to work drafting and redrafting the necessary documents. At three in the morning the papers were ready for signature. Purvis hesitated briefly before he signed. He was accepting $500m of obligations for the British Government. There was no time to consult London again. The whole deal might fall through at any moment.

No wonder he was nervous. This was a complete reversal of the careful spending policy the British had followed to make their dollars last, but now, if Britain was to fight on, it was all or nothing. Purvis told his friends later it was the biggest decision of his life.

Barely five hours after the documents were signed, all French assets in the US were frozen. Purvis was not sure that the American manufacturers would accept the documents. He approached a few American companies to get their reaction. There was some hesitation at first. Then Donald Douglas, president of Douglas Aircraft Company, accepted it and the rest fell in line. The arms that had been destined for the French would now pass to the British.[13] Purvis' efforts were instrumental in ensuring that Britain had the resources to continue the fight in 1940.

The rifles and aircraft that were to be provided to Britain were useful, but Churchill still hankered after the American destroyers to protect the country's vital economic lifelines to the Empire and Dominions on which so much of Britain's wealth and status depended. Fortunately for Churchill, the United States was equally concerned about protecting itself and wanted offshore bases for its own defence. Britain had possessions in suitable locations.

---

13 Sadly, Arthur Purvis was not to live to see the outcome of his efforts. He died in an air crash on 14 August 1941, shortly after taking off from RAF Heathfield in Scotland.

Although the ingredients of a mutually beneficial deal were present, the conclusion of an agreement was delayed by political and legal considerations. Once again Arthur Purvis played a key role. President Roosevelt finally decided he could transfer the destroyers if he could portray the deal as designed to improve US national defence. Roosevelt also requested a pledge from Churchill that if Britain fell, the Royal Navy would not be surrendered but would carry on the fight from ports in the British Empire. The promises, Roosevelt explained, were 'molasses to sweeten the pill in America'. (*Reynolds, 1988*)

When the British Cabinet received the proposal, its first reaction was to refuse. The War Cabinet minutes read: 'The view of the War Cabinet was that a formal bargain on the lines proposed was out of the question.' (Reynolds, 1988)

Even Churchill was against giving what he called 'a blank cheque on the whole of our transatlantic possessions' (Reynolds, 1988), but Britain did not hold the upper hand and Churchill had little choice but to accept aid on whatever terms America proposed.

On 2 September 1940 the 'Destroyers for Bases' deal was signed. It was of symbolic as well as practical importance. The United States was formally neutral and yet, with this act, it had effectively pledged support for Britain as America's own front line of defence. In return, the deal gave the United States the right to establish bases at Newfoundland and Bermuda, and six additional sites in the Caribbean.

The exchange was well received in Britain, where Churchill emphasised that the destroyers were a gift. In the USA, Roosevelt portrayed the exchange as a swap of old ships for strong bases: a 'generous action ... to enhance the national security of the United States'.[14]

The English songwriters Billy Ayerst and Hughie Charles adapted an earlier American song written by Morris H. Rosenfeld and Alfred J. Lawrence in 1933 that expressed gratitude to Roosevelt for his New Deal policies. This British version reflected the popular public sentiment in 1940:

---

14 The deal that Roosevelt approved provided for the immediate transfer of fifty Caldwell, Wickes, and Clemson-class US Navy destroyers, referred to as the 'twelve-hundred-ton type'. Forty-three ships initially went to the Royal Navy and seven to the Royal Canadian Navy. In exchange, the US was granted land in various British possessions for the establishment of naval or air bases with rent-free, nineteen-year leases.

So, we say 'thanks Mr. Roosevelt'
It's swell of you for the way.
you're helping us to carry on.
you'll see the British Empire smiling through.
when these dark and stormy days are gone

and Franklin, by the way, please convey.
our congratulations to the folks in USA
we're saying 'thanks Mr Roosevelt we're proud of you.
for the way you're helping us to carry on'.[15]

The destroyers were duly transferred to the Royal Navy at the end of 1940, but it was soon discovered that they required significant maintenance and refitting before they could be deployed. It was not until well into 1941 that they were able to make a significant contribution to convoy escort operations.

The picture presented by Winston Churchill to the British (and American) people of the nation standing alone after the fall of France was hugely powerful and he used the image repeatedly in his speeches and in his dealings with Roosevelt. However, it was an exaggeration, nonetheless. In June 1940, the British Empire controlled Crown colonies and protectorates in every continent. It also maintained strong political ties with Australia, Canada, South Africa and New Zealand. In Europe, Britain was on its own but in the wider world, Commonwealth, Colonial and Imperial Indian forces totalled close to 15 million serving men and women and the British Empire and the Commonwealth had direct or de facto political and economic control of 25 per cent of the world's population, and of 30 per cent of its land mass.[16] These Colonial forces were to play a key role in the battles that were to come.

However, after Dunkirk, Churchill was in desperate need of a British propaganda success. The target for an airborne operation in south-east Italy had first been suggested by Professor Colin Hardie,[17] a fellow of Magdalene College, Oxford, who had been seconded to the War Office. He came up with the idea of targeting a viaduct in Italy:

---

15 The song was recorded by Joy Nichol (Columbia DB 1715) and by George Formby (Regal Zonophone MR 1950).

16 The sacrifices made by the Colonies and Commonwealth are often overlooked in Britain. These nations suffered 150,000 military deaths, 400,000 wounded, 100,000 prisoners, over 300,000 civilian deaths, and the loss of seventy major warships, thirty-nine submarines, 3,500 aircraft, 1,100 tanks and 65,000 vehicles.

17 Colin Hardie was also a member of the Inklings, the informal literary discussion group that included J.R.R. Tolkien and C.S. Lewis, among others.

> The water supply of the whole area of south-east Italy … is derived from one aqueduct, the Aqueduct Pugliese. If that aqueduct, snaking through Italy's Apennine Mountains, could be severed, two to three million people and two vital naval bases, Taranto and Brindisi, would be starved of water. (*Buckingham*, 2008)

It is sobering to imagine the reserved academic who loved Virgil, the city of Rome and the Italian language should have dreamt up a plan that may have resulted in the deaths of many thousands of ordinary Italians, but it was just the sort of daring plan that Churchill had been looking for.

The mission, which was planned for February 1941, was designed to showcase the ability of the RAF to deliver men and equipment accurately by parachute. The operation was given the code name *Colossus* and was to be the very first British airborne raid. Anthony Deane-Drummond, who was one of the officers selected for the raid, wrote: 'Our excitement can be imagined, and we all congratulated ourselves on our good fortune in having been chosen for the job from the whole Commando.' (Buckingham, 2008)

It is, perhaps, surprising that none of those involved questioned the morality of the mission. The justification was that Mussolini had declared war on Britain on 10 June 1940, and had launched air raids against Malta on the following day, but does one wrong justify another? War makes savages of us all.

I knew an Italian civilian who took part in this raid. His name was Fortunato Picchi, and he worked as under-banqueting manager at the Savoy Hotel, where he was known as 'Little Fortune'. Picchi had come to Britain in 1920 and had been interned as an enemy alien in the initial stages of the Second World War, but he had impressed Military Intelligence by his anti-fascist views and his willingness to join the British war effort. He was recruited by the SOE to accompany the raiding party as an Italian interpreter. Picchi had applied to become a British citizen immediately before the raid, but he knew full well that if he was captured he would be deemed a traitor to Italy and would face certain death.

The raiding party flew directly to Malta and from there they were parachuted into southern Italy. The demolition party made their way to the viaduct, laid the explosives and then took shelter nearby. After the dust had settled it appeared that the mission had been successful, and half the aqueduct was down. The raiders were then divided into three groups to make their way independently to the coast, where the Royal Navy submarine HMS *Triumph* would be waiting to collect them.

Unfortunately, their plan of marching 50 miles across mountainous terrain in wintry conditions was over-ambitious and the men were captured by the Italian forces.

Shackled together with a long chain, the party was made to march to Teora, accompanied by the shouts of angry Italians, threatening to lynch them. They were then taken to the Poggioreale civilian prison in Naples, where they were interrogated first by the Italians and later by the Germans. They were then taken to a PoW. camp at Sulmona. Once Picchi was identified, he was separated from the others, and transferred to Rome, where he was held at Regina Coeli Prison. Here he was tried, found guilty of treason, and executed by firing squad.

On the evening of 12 February 1941, the Italian authorities gloated over the failure of the raid and the capture of the men, forcing the Ministry of Information to confirm the bare details of the operation. The British forces, under Churchill's unrealistic urgings, had overreached themselves. *The Times* presented the raiders as martyrs to the British war effort. When I read about Picchi's fate in the *Daily Herald* I was less than convinced. It seemed to me that a good and innocent man had been sacrificed for nothing. (*Daily Herald*, 1941)

Once the US elections of 1941 were out of the way, Roosevelt became more open in his support of Britain against the Axis powers, but he remained determined to avoid the USA becoming directly involved in the war. Claude Pepper, a Democrat senator, admitted that he saw Britain as 'a sort of mercenary: as a way of defending America by keeping it out of the war, doing America's fighting for her'. (*Reynolds*, 1988) At the centre of this strategy was the policy of 'Lend-Lease'.

In 1917 President Wilson had been drawn into the war against Germany because of attacks on American shipping in the North Atlantic. In 1941 it seemed possible that this would happen again as Germany's U-boat fleet was becoming increasingly successful. In April 1941, Roosevelt issued orders that the American navy should be ready to escort Allied convoys across the North Atlantic, but at the last moment he drew back in response to domestic opposition.

Meanwhile, Britain was becoming increasingly demoralised by military setbacks in Greece and North Africa. There were fears that once Hitler had achieved dominance in the Mediterranean he would turn once again to the invasion of Britain. For the first time since the dark days of June 1940 Churchill pleaded with Roosevelt to enter the war. On 4 May 1941, he cabled: 'Mr President, I am sure you will not misunderstand me if I speak to you exactly what is in my mind.' (Reynolds, 1988)

However, Roosevelt remained firmly against leading his people into war, convinced that it would only be possible when Hitler challenged American interests to the extent that national unity would be guaranteed. That challenge was finally delivered not by Germany but by Japan. Germany's surprise attack on Russia convinced the Japanese that Stalin would not be able to resist their expansion in Asia. Furthermore, Britain was unable to spare forces for Singapore and Malaya or ships to patrol the China Seas. Only the Americans, with their main fleet at Pearl Harbor in Hawaii, offered any deterrent to Japanese expansion in south-east Asia.

In July 1941 Japan overran the remainder of French Indochina (which included modern-day Vietnam, Laos and Cambodia). This occupation had significant geopolitical consequences as it prompted America, Britain, and the Netherlands to freeze Japanese assets and impose an oil embargo on Japan. This embargo severely threatened Japan's access to vital resources, pushing the country closer to its decision to launch further military actions in the Pacific.

By December it was expected that Japan would mount an attack on British and Dutch possessions in south-east Asia, but the bombing of Pearl Harbor on the morning of 7 December 1941 came as a complete shock. The attack resulted in the sinking or immobilising of eight American battleships and the deaths of 2,400 American sailors. It was the most humiliating military disaster in American history.

On the eve of Pearl Harbor the Chairman of the New York Chapter of America First Committee, who opposed American involvement in the war, had sent a long critical letter to Roosevelt. When the extent of the destruction at Pearl Harbor became apparent, he wrote again: 'Please consider the contents of our letter, dated 6 December 1941, null and void.' (*Reynolds, 1988*)

After America declared war on Japan, Adolf Hitler declared war on America on 11 December 1941. There were several reasons behind this decision. Firstly, Germany, Italy and Japan were part of the Tripartite Pact.[18] This was a defensive alliance and although it did not oblige Germany to declare war if Japan attacked another country, Hitler chose to support his ally. In doing so he cited a number of provocations by the United States, including the Lend-Lease Act and the US Navy's involvement in escorting convoys and engaging German U-boats.

18 Several other countries joined the pact later: Hungary (20 November 1940), Romania (23 November 1940), Slovakia (24 November 1940), Bulgaria (1 March 1941), Yugoslavia (25 March 1941) and Croatia (15 June 1941).

After Hitler's declaration of war, Roosevelt cabled Churchill: 'Today all of us are in the same boat with you and the people of the Empire, and it is a ship which will not and cannot be sunk.' (*Reynolds, 1988*)

Churchill was jubilant. He recalled later, 'I went to bed and slept the sleep of the saved and thankful.' (*Mawdsley, 2012*)

If Churchill's first reaction to Pearl Harbor was relief, he soon became worried that America might prioritise the defeat of Japan over the defeat of Germany. The attack on Pearl Harbor was followed by successful Japanese assaults on the Philippines, Malaya, Singapore, Burma and the Dutch East Indies – victories that tipped the balance of power in the Pacific. Powerful voices, particularly in the American Navy, urged Roosevelt to concentrate on the Pacific and leave the Atlantic to Britain. Throughout the war these tensions persisted.

The diary of Alan Brooke, the British Chief of the Imperial General Staff, records that the day after America's entry into the war one of the British chiefs urged that a more deferential tone to the USA should be adopted to keep them on side. Winston Churchill replied: 'Oh! That is the way we talked to her while we were wooing her; now that she is in the harem, we talk to her quite differently.' (*Bryant, 1957*)

Chapter 6

GENESIS OF THE ITALIAN CAMPAIGN

It was the Arcadia Conference that cemented the relationship between Britain and the USA and which lead to the events that would change my life.

The Arcadia Conference (also known as the First Washington Conference), took place from 22 December 1941 to 14 January 1942, in Washington, D.C. The build-up to this conference was the urgent need for coordination between the Allies to align their war efforts.

The British and American military leaders had different strategic priorities. The British were focused on maintaining their lines of communication with the colonies, while the Americans were split. The US Navy wanted to prioritise the Pacific war against Japan while the US Army, led by General George C. Marshall, the Commanding General of the Field Forces and Chief of Staff, US Army, advocated an immediate cross-Channel invasion of Europe.

Despite the risks posed by German U-boats in the Atlantic, Churchill decided to travel to Washington, D.C., to meet Roosevelt. Churchill arrived in Washington in time for Christmas 1941, appearing with Roosevelt on the steps of the White House to turn on the Christmas lights.

Churchill was an eccentric and demanding houseguest, and according to the White House butler who had been allocated to him, Churchill said to him:

> Now, Fields, we had a lovely dinner last night, but I have a few orders for you. We want to leave here as friends, right? I must have a tumbler of sherry in my room before breakfast, a couple of glasses of scotch

> and soda before lunch and French champagne, and 90-year-old brandy before I go to sleep at night. (*Stelzer, 2012*)

Roosevelt was not in the best of health. He had been diagnosed with polio in 1921, which left him with significant mobility issues, and he was also suffering from heart disease and hypertension. To Eleanor Roosevelt's exasperation, Churchill kept her husband up until 2 or 3 a.m. drinking brandy, smoking cigars and ignoring her urgings to get some sleep. She later wrote: 'It was astonishing to me that anyone could smoke so much and drink so much and keep perfectly well.' (*Pilpel, 1976*) Harold Ickes, who was Roosevelt's interior secretary, noted in his diary, that the President had remarked that Churchill was 'drunk half of his time'. (*Ickes, 1955*)

All the decisions made at Arcadia were kept secret, other than the 'Declaration by United Nations', which committed the Allies to make no separate peace with the enemy, and to use all their resources until victory was achieved. The main policy decision reached at Arcadia was that a Combined Chiefs of Staff, based in Washington, should be created.

A key mover in this agreement was George Marshall. As a member of John J. Pershing's staff he had witnessed the squabbles between the Americans, British and French during the Great War, when Pershing had resisted British and French demands that American forces be integrated with their armies.

Marshall highlighted the benefits of having a single commander in each theatre who would have authority over all ground, naval and air forces. Marshall provided practical examples of how a unified command could work effectively, emphasising the need for a coordinated approach to tackle the complex challenges of the war. Field Marshal Sir John Dill, who had a good working relationship with Marshall, played a significant role in bridging the gap between the British and American military perspectives. Their efforts at the Arcadia Conference changed the course of the war.

The man selected as the single commander of British and American forces in the Mediterranean was Harold Alexander, a British career soldier who rose to prominence in the Great War and who had overseen the final stages of the Allied evacuation from Dunkirk. To many of his fellow officers, Alexander was a heroic figure: handsome, mannered and immaculately dressed, but others found him remote and hard to get to know.

It was agreed that the US General, Dwight Eisenhower, would head up the Combined Chiefs of Staff and would resolve problems of strategy and logistics under the direction of Roosevelt and Churchill. Other combined bodies were created to handle munitions, shipping, raw materials, food and production.

This alliance was quite different from the arm's-length association of 1917–18, let alone the distrust and suspicion of the 1930s. As Marshall remarked later, it was 'the most complete unification of military effort ever achieved by two Allied nations'. (*US News and World Report*, 1945)

Churchill returned to Britain in January 1942 pleased that the conference confirmed his conviction that: 'Notwithstanding the entry of Japan into the War, our view remains that Germany is still the prime enemy and her defeat is the key to victory. Once Germany is defeated, the collapse of Italy and the defeat of Japan must follow.' (*Higgins, 1957*)

A decision on where to commit American troops to battle had not yet been taken but to demonstrate his commitment, Roosevelt sent the first American troops to Britain within weeks. Churchill told the King that: 'After months of walking out together, Britain and America were now married.' (*Reynolds, 1988*)

However, the new relationship could not disguise the fact that there was still a fundamental disagreement between Britain and America over the best strategy for winning the war. The American leaders still wanted a cross-Channel invasion at the first opportunity and to them (and to Stalin), Churchill seemed unnecessarily cautious.

In April 1942 Marshall arrived in London with fresh proposals for a massive build-up of a million US troops in Britain over the coming year, backed by airfields, supply depots and other support facilities. The aim was a full-scale Anglo-American invasion of France the following summer (code-named Operation Round-Up). Marshall also wanted cross-Channel raids throughout 1942 and entertained the possibility of an emergency invasion that year if either Russia or Germany seemed on the verge of collapse. Marshall's message was clear: 'Through France passes our shortest route to the heart of Germany.' (*Eiler, 1987*)

However, the British leaders thought that this plan was over-ambitious and unrealistic. Alan Brooke told the Americans: 'We are all completely in agreement as regards 1943, but if we were forced this year to undertake an operation on the Continent, it could only be on a small scale.' (*Bruce, 1987*)

Privately Brooke had doubts. He thought that America had insufficient battle-ready troops, and that British forces were tied down in North Africa and the Far East. He maintained that the Americans had little idea of the immense logistical problems that would be involved in a cross-Channel invasion.

Churchill, on the other hand, took the more pragmatic view that Britain could not afford to fall out with the Americans at such a crucial time, particularly as Roosevelt in a personal letter to Churchill had made it clear that Marshall's plan 'has my heart and mind in it'. (*Gelb, 1992*)

Brooke's doubts were therefore swept under the carpet and Churchill cabled the President: 'I am in entire agreement in principle with all you propose, and so are the Chiefs of Staff.' (*Nisbet, 1988*)

However, Marshall was not fooled. In the Boeing 314 Clipper flying boat that took him back to Washington, Marshall turned to his senior army planner and said, 'I think the British have bought your plan, but I think they did so with their tongues in their cheek.' (*Reynolds, 1988*)

Marshall was right to be sceptical. In June 1942, Churchill declared that: 'No assault could be mounted this year.' (*Gilbert, 1966*).

Under pressure from Stalin, Roosevelt and Churchill both agreed that it was necessary to open a second front somewhere in Europe during 1942, even if a cross-Channel invasion of France was not practicable. Roosevelt was concerned that the American public were clamouring for an all-out assault on Japan as revenge for Pearl Harbor. They could see why America was fighting the Japanese but were less clear why they were fighting the Germans in Europe. Unless decisions were made soon, the pressure for a major assault in the Pacific would become too strong to withstand.

Churchill's proposal to Roosevelt was for an invasion of Algeria and Tunisia. British troops had their backs to the wall in Egypt, so such an initiative would relieve this pressure. Marshall and General Albert Wedemeyer were appalled. They were convinced that if the Allies diverted their resources to the Mediterranean, it would make it impossible to invade France in 1943, but Roosevelt overruled them and sided with Churchill.

The divide in strategy widened with Churchill's increasing enthusiasm for an invasion of Italy. He first used the phrase 'soft underbelly' in a meeting with Joseph Stalin in the summer of 1942 when trying to convince him that his plan for a second front in North Africa and Italy would be better than a cross-Channel invasion. To illustrate his point, Churchill used his skill as an artist to draw Stalin a picture of a crocodile with a hard exterior and a soft white tummy. What he did not confess to Stalin was that he was still bruised by the criticisms he had received for his part of the Great War battles in Salonika and he believed implicitly that the strategy of attacking what he perceived to be the weaker front had been the right one, despite the disasters of the Dardanelles and Gallipoli and the three years of attritional warfare that preceded victory in the Balkans.[19] He told Stalin:

> The great prize when Sicily falls is to get Italy out of the war. Bulgaria's defeatism in 1918 brought about the collapse of Germany; might not Italy's surrender now have similar consequences? It will surely cause a chill of loneliness to settle on the German people and might very well be the beginning of the end. (*Wilson, 1966*)

However, there was more to it than that. Churchill maintained a romantic view of Greece as the cradle of democracy and Rome as the Eternal City. He saw the freeing of these two ancient Mediterranean cities as central to the battle between civilisation and the barbarians. Warming to his own rhetoric, he repeated the 'soft underbelly of the Axis' phrase in a speech at Mansion House in November 1942, but when Roosevelt was asked what he thought of Churchill's plan, he answered: 'Not much'.

The Americans had become convinced that Churchill's principal obsession was to keep the Suez Canal secure for Britain and maintain its traditional influence in the Middle East. Wedemeyer told Marshall that British plans 'have been designed to maintain the integrity of the British Empire and would lead to the Allies' total defeat in Europe and Asia'. General Eisenhower predicted that Roosevelt's decision to back Churchill's plan against the advice of his military planners could well be the 'blackest day in history'.

The US Secretary of War, Henry Stimson, was similarly opposed to Churchill's plan, but his objection was that Churchill was just too timid and that: 'The British preference was for picking off its allies and bombing its cities into ruin.' The American Admiral Ernest King agreed and put it even more scathingly: 'the British would only invade the Continent when there was no resistance left and they could march in behind a Scotch bagpipe band'. He saw no clear role for the US Navy in Europe under Churchill's plan and pressed repeatedly for supplies to be diverted to the Pacific.

What particularly annoyed the Americans was the ability of the British to get their own way with Roosevelt, but the Americans were at a disadvantage of being uncoordinated. Brooke and his colleagues were often dismayed by Churchill's obstinacy and his 'midnight

19 Churchill had used the phrase 'naked belly' in the Great War when referring to the border of the Austro-Hungarian empire in the Balkans.

follies', but any disagreements were aired behind closed doors so that when the British arrived at conferences, they had agreed their position in advance. By contrast, the policy making of the Americans was haphazard. Roosevelt frequently failed to consult his Joint Chiefs and sometimes argued with them in front of the British.

However, even as the Americans were being ground down, the British side was not quite as unified as it appeared. Brooke remained doubtful about whether Italy really was a 'soft underbelly' and argued that a more limited action in Sardinia might yield comparable results at less cost. Churchill was in no mood to give ground now that he had Roosevelt on side and, wounded by American suggestions that he was timid, he became more bold and more forthright about his ambitions, nagging Brooke (or 'Brookie' as he called him) with complaints that: 'Everywhere the British and Americans are overloading their operational plans with so many factors of safety that they are ceasing to be capable of making any form of aggressive warfare.' (*Trumbull, 1968*)

Churchill was now utterly convinced that he was in the right and he was itching to launch a full-scale invasion of Sicily.

Chapter 7

WAITING FOR MY CALL-UP PAPERS

As I waited anxiously for my call-up papers, an exciting new opportunity arose for me when my cousin, who was a stage manager at the Prince's Theatre in Shaftesbury Avenue, offered me a job as a stagehand working on a revival of Jerome Kern's *Wild Rose*. The show, which opened on my twentieth birthday on 14 August 1942 starred Jessie Mathews singing her most famous number 'Look for the Silver Lining'. I saw her every day in rehearsals, and I think she took a bit of a fancy to me! I had the time of my life.

Once the job ended, I needed something else to do. I saw an advertisement in the paper for men to help clear up the destruction caused to the city of Bristol in the blitz in the previous year.[20] Although I had no previous experience of the demolition business, I was strong and fit and thought that this might even get me out of military service when my time came. I talked it over with my friend and cousin Dinny Neil, who was still living with his parents at Charlton Street. He was bored with his job as a sign writer, and he agreed to come with me to Bristol.

We soon found work in Bristol knocking down buildings damaged by German bombs. With its harbour and its aircraft factories, Bristol had been a prime target and was easily found as enemy bombers were able to trace a course up the River Avon.

For a time, we were footloose and enjoying our freedom. We were both good-looking 20-year-olds and I went out a few times with a young girl who worked in a baker's shop and who always managed to

20 The Bristol Blitz was between November 1940 and April 1941. Bristol was the fifth-most heavily bombed British city of the war and 90,000 buildings were bomb damaged.

slip me an extra bun. I enjoyed the demolition work. I had no fear of heights in those days. One day, our gang was called to a seriously bomb-damaged warehouse with just one remaining wall poised precariously above a busy street. There was no chance of getting a crane to the site and so the foremen called for a volunteer to scale the wall to demolish it brick by-brick using a sledgehammer. None of the other boys fancied the task, so I stepped forward.

News of the demolition attracted the attention of a press photographer. The photograph of me swinging the sledgehammer while standing precariously on the apex of the wall and silhouetted against the Bristol sky was published in an article headlined 'hero of the blitz' in the *Daily Mail*.[21]

For a while we were happy in Bristol until our demolition gang was called upon to make safe a severely damaged Roman Catholic church. When we arrived on the site, one of our gang spotted the large quantity of lead flashing from the church roof that lay among the ruins. He carried the lead away, intending to sell it for scrap. I had no knowledge of this and would never have done something like this in a Catholic church of all places, but he did. When the priest discovered the theft, he cursed us publicly. Even though I was not involved, I carried that curse with me and still believe it was the cause of my subsequent misfortune.

I was never a conscientious objector, but the Irish premier had declared that Ireland would remain neutral in this war and like many members of the Anglo-Irish community I had no overwhelming desire to join the British armed forces. However, I knew it was only a matter of time before I would be called up and, in September 1942, my papers arrived with an order stating:

> If you fail to comply with this order, the police will be informed of your absence. You should arrive at the barracks early rather than late in the day, using the travel warrant enclosed for the railway journey. Bring along your razor and toothbrush. Also, a travelling case for returning your civilian clothes back to your home address.

My cousin and I then came up with a scheme that was so hare-brained, I don't know why we ever thought we could get away with it. He told me:

21 This story was confirmed to me in person by Dinny Neil in 1999.

> Look, we've both got the same name and were both born in the same year so why don't you take my papers, and I'll take yours, then we can both pretend that there has been a mix-up. They will eventually sort it out, but that will take time.

Dinny duly reported to the recruitment office, presenting my papers and declaring that a mistake had been made. I left Bristol and went home to Drury Lane. Our little scheme worked for all of five minutes. Dinny was pressed into service regardless and the following day, I was arrested by red caps from the Royal Military Police in the Royal Opera House, which was being used as a dancehall. I was taken back to Bow Street Police Station, just round the corner from my home in Drury Lane.

In the Police Court it was established that I had no case for not joining the Army, and I was taken from Bow Street to the cells in the Old War Office building in Whitehall. My punishment was five days behind bars before being assigned to a front-line infantry unit with the promise of being moved into battle immediately I had completed my training.

Chapter 8

ARRIVAL IN COLCHESTER

Author's Note: Much of the detail of the training that I underwent at Colchester and Mundesley is drawn from the memoires of David Ivan Vere, who arrived at Colchester on the same day as me and trained with me until we were both posted to Italy. David's son has kindly agreed that I may supplement my memories with details that I have long since forgotten but which David recorded in his excellent book *Give Us This Day* that was published by Author House in 2006.

Having served my sentence, I was taken by red caps from the Old War Office building to Liverpool Street Station, which was already crowded with men in Army uniform and many more in civilian clothes obviously heading for military service. After a short wait, we boarded a train that made many stops along the way, before finally pulling into Colchester Station.

Waiting for us in the station yard were several lorries with the drivers calling out the names of various barracks. I was told that I had been assigned to Meanee Barracks and so I climbed up into the lorry full of men ranging in age from 19 to their mid-30s. It soon pulled off, passing through Colchester town, up a slight hill, and then through the large wrought iron gates of the Meanee Barracks on the outskirts of the town.

Inside the gates, there were two-storey accommodation blocks on one side of a wide road with small buildings on the other side. After climbing down from the lorry, we were ordered to form up in a line outside a reception building. We then filed in and were asked to give our details to two officials. We had to supply our next of kin, religious denomination, last job and some other details that I now forget. At the end of the process, I was given a slip of paper bearing my service number. A number I will never forget: 5683130.

Waiting outside the reception block there was a growing group of men who would be training with me in the same platoon. We were taken to our quarters on the ground floor of one of the accommodation blocks filled with forty bunk beds. The lance corporal, who was the NCO in charge of our block, then marched us to the mess hall for the midday meal. Any enthusiasm for food after the long journey to Colchester soon disappeared when I saw the ladle of grey stew and half a slice of stale bread that was dumped on to my plate. Sitting down at one of the mess tables with my new companions, I was in no mood for talking – and nor were they. None of us felt any enthusiasm for what was in front of us.

After the meal was over, we formed up outside and marched back to our quarters, where we found the platoon sergeant waiting for us. He told us that we must always address him as 'sergeant' and always stand to attention when speaking with an NCO or an officer. He went on to say that we must always salute an officer and never speak to an officer unless spoken to. Already it seemed like too many petty rules for my liking.

We were told that the next six weeks would be taken up with basic infantry training: in small arms, drill and fieldcraft. Sensing that a few of us were allowing our minds to wander, he barked at us:

> Always pay attention to what I tell you if you want to keep your name off the village war memorial! You have no rights in the Army. Your only entitlement is to be given three meals a day, pay and leave. See this book: this is the King's Rules and Regulations, which you must learn and comply with. Everything you receive here is a privilege. Don't forget to listen to the bugle calls in the camp, and recognise the different calls played: 'reveille', 'mess calls', 'fire picket' and 'lights out'. Lastly, if any of you men feel unfit for duty, you must first notify an NCO to place your name on sick report for sick parade. You will be issued with your Army kit tomorrow and you will need to get your civilian clothes posted home. I can't have you going around like a rabble. (*Vere, 2006*)

After this little lecture, he took us on a guided tour of the camp, beginning at the main gate and the guardhouse, telling us to make sure that we didn't end up in there. Having been in a cell in London, this was advice that I was keen to heed. We moved on, and we were shown the barber's shop, armoury, rifle range, the straw shed and a building containing a gas chamber. We were told that we would all have to pass through it as part of the training.

Once the tour of the camp was over, we went back to our billet. The sergeant then called us to attention and walked along the backs of the three ranks of men, tapping some of them on the shoulder with a firm command of 'haircut'. I had a shock of brown curly hair, but it was cut neat, and I stood there in complete confidence that the sergeant would pass by without touching me on the shoulder until I suddenly heard the word 'haircut' yelled into my right ear. My first reaction was to tell him to 'f... off', but the thought of the cells stopped me, and I didn't say a word.

With several others, I was marched off to the camp barber shop, a dingy place, with none of the trappings of my barbers in *Drury Lane*. When my turn came round, I sat in the chair and the barber wrapped a cloth around my neck and shoulders. Taking up his very blunt cut-throat razor, he set to work on the back of my neck. The burning sensation was painful, but once again, the thought of the guardhouse prevented me from speaking out. However, I decided there and then that in future I would have my hair cut in Colchester.

After I had had my hair cut, the sergeant moved to the front of the platoon and told us that the corporal would now take us over to the straw shed to get our thin mattresses filled. The corporal told us not to stuff in too much straw because it would form into clumps that would be uncomfortable for sleeping on. It was just like being back hop picking!

We were then marched off to our tea of bread, margarine and jam, a thin slice of fruitcake and weak tea served in an enamel pint mug. After eating, the corporal had us form up outside before we were marched back to what was to be our new home for the next six weeks.

At the billet, the corporal called out the names of each man from a register. Finding we were all present and correct, he then ran through more rules and regulations telling us that we must read the company orders every day for any duties we had been given. These orders were posted on a noticeboard under the heading: 'Read and Digest Thoroughly!'

Next to the noticeboard was the toilet, which had no hot water and just one cold water tap. We had to shave in this washroom every morning before first parade at 6.30 a.m. With reveille at 6 a.m., this meant that there was only thirty minutes for all of us to wash, shave and make our beds.

We were then told that we must not try to leave the camp for any reason as we were all confined to barracks until we had had our inoculations and vaccinations. We were told to use the time to work on our kit, polishing the brass work and the webbing, and giving our boots a coat of dubbin.

By the time of lights out at 10 p.m. we had made our beds with the three Army blankets provided, and a round bolster that served as a pillow. The straw in the mattresses rustled noisily as the men got settled in their beds. I found it hard to sleep that night. I was used to sleeping in a room with others, but my fellow recruits were an exceptionally noisy bunch!

After a fitful night's sleep, the light blazed on in the room at 6 a.m. with the bugler sounding 'reveille' and we were soon out of our beds and on our feet. I managed to get a place in the washroom and started shaving in the cold water. It was not pleasant.

At 6.30 a.m. the corporal told us to form a semicircle round a table. He then moved to his bunk and from underneath it he pulled out a Bren gun that he had retrieved from the armoury. He then explained about the use of the Bren gun and its role in an infantry section. He explained that the Bren gun was a British version of a Czechoslovak light machine gun that had a distinctive top-mounted, curved box magazine. The corporal explained that the Bren gun was operated by a two-man crew, and a lance corporal who made up a 'gun group'. Men who were not assigned to a gun group were allocated to 'rifle groups'.

In the gun groups, the Number 1 gunner carried and fired the Bren gun, while the Number 2 loader loaded the gun and carried extra magazines, a spare barrel that could be quickly changed when the original one became hot during sustained fire, and a tool kit. The Number 2 was also responsible for spotting targets.

It was explained to us that the Bren gun was usually fired from a prone position using a two-legged stand. It was a gas-operated weapon using the same .303 ammunition as the standard British bolt-action rifle, SMLE (Short Magazine Lee Enfield), and could fire at a rate of around 500 rounds per minute. The Bren gun had a range of around 550m when fired like that. The magazine that was mounted at the top of the gun used to vibrate and move when it was being fired, making the weapon more visible, and many Bren gunners used paint or canvas covers to disguise it. We were also told that in a battle situation single shot should sometimes be fired in imitation of rifle fire to conceal its presence.

After the lesson with the Bren gun, we were marched off for breakfast, which comprised porridge with salt and one sausage with beans. Later in the morning, and still in our civilian clothing, we were marched to the camp's administration building where, in exchange for our civilian identity cards, Army clerks issued us with our pay books.[22]

---

22 Officially designated *Army Book 64: The Soldier's Service and pay books, part one and two.*

After we had received our pay-books we were sent to the medical officer and ordered to stand in single file with our coats off and shirt sleeves rolled well up, ready for an inoculation in both arms. The corporal warned us again about leaving the camp. We were then all placed on light duties over the weekend to give us a chance to recover from any side effects from our jabs.

After our midday meal, we were told to parade at the quartermaster's stores at 2 p.m. to collect our kit. We filed inside and reformed into three ranks. The quartermaster was there together with his orderly storemen waiting behind a counter with racks piled high with stores. The quartermaster told us to take care of the articles we were being issued with: 'They cost a great deal of money and have to be paid for by the taxpayers in the country.' I think he half expected us to be grateful for these 'gifts'.

The first man in line went to the counter and was given a kit bag, and proceeded down the counter accompanied by an orderly, who called out the man's size just by looking at him. Having returned to the billet with our overloaded kit bags, the corporal told us to get changed into our new serge battledress jackets and trousers. I then took off my smart, colourful shirt and neck scarf and replaced them with the drab army uniform. I mumbled to myself: 'Well if you didn't know it before, you do now: you're in the Army, Den.'

I packed my own clothes away in my suitcase that was to be sent home to my mother. I had already prepared a brief note home with the address of the barracks, and I put this inside the case. When all the cases were ready, they were collected by the postman in a GPO van later that afternoon and taken down to Colchester station.

The following morning, which was a Saturday, we were marched to breakfast looking like a bunch of soldiers. After breakfast, we were required to do a long session of drill to help us learn to move as a unit and respond to the commands: 'Attention,' 'Stand at ease,' and 'Dismissed' to ensure that we could form up, move, and stand correctly. It was tedious stuff. When, at last, the parade ended we had nothing to do but polish the toecaps of our boots and the brass on our webbing. For the first time, we started to chat to each other and started to form some kind of friendships.

At teatime, we strolled over to the cookhouse, where we were surprised to find a slightly more appetising meal than we were usually given. At 6 p.m. we were even allowed to light the coal fire in the billet and the rest of the evening was spent talking round the fire. Later that evening I wrote a letter home, and then read my book until lights out.

Chapter 9

REPORTING FOR DUTIES

On Sunday morning, we reported at the officers' mess for our duties. At the door of the mess, the orderly sergeant was waiting for us, wearing his red sash. He barked at us to wipe our boots and take our caps off and then led us into a large hallway. I was ordered to report to the kitchen, where I was given a bucket of hot water and soap, scrubbing brushes and cloths. Getting down on my knees, I had to remove the dried mud from the tiled floor. It was demanding work for what they called 'light duties'. After Sunday dinner and back in our billet, the corporal told us that the platoon officer would probably be coming soon and that the real training was about to start.

As a Roman Catholic, I was excused from the church parade and allowed to walk to St James the Less & St Helen Church in the centre of Colchester. The rest of the evening was spent talking round the fire. Like most of the men, I was in my bunk long before lights out.

On Monday morning, after the first parade and breakfast, we were ordered outside for drill. The sergeant then marched us on to the main parade ground where other platoons were being drilled. Our sergeant demonstrated the correct way to drill, and gave us the orders: 'Stand at ease'; 'Attention'; 'By the Left'; 'Quick march'; 'Left right'; 'Move to the left in diagonal march'; 'Left incline'; Right incline'; 'About turn'. He said, 'That's how it should be done and that's how I want it done.'

The drill started and went very well at first, that is until one of the men got confused between his left and right, moving the wrong way and making the platoon just fold up on itself with the men aimlessly walking about trying to re-form the broken ranks. The sergeant was now very angry and red-faced: 'As you were! Fall back into three ranks and look sharp about it!' Once the platoon had sorted itself out and was back standing to attention, the sergeant gave us a dressing down for our incompetence. He told us the answer was more drill, so back we went to pounding the parade ground. Our only consolation was that we could hear that the other platoons were having similar problems.

A young second lieutenant then arrived on the parade ground. The sergeant called us to a halt and, after an exchange of salutes and a few quick words together, the sergeant turned back to us and gave the order: 'For inspection; open order march; eyes right; straighten the line; front rank, arm's length from next man; eyes front; Stand still.' The sergeant turned back to the officer, saluted him, and shouted, 'Platoon ready for your inspection, sir!' The officer then walked along the three ranks of men, sometimes stopping to speak.

With the inspection over, the officer and the sergeant walked back to the front of the platoon, about turned and faced us. The sergeant then gave us the order: 'Close order march; Keep still.' Then with a return of salutes again, the officer walked off the parade ground.

Later that day, all of us new recruits were issued with our identity discs. These came in pairs and were made of fibre. They bore the name, number and religion of the owner. The two disks were joined together with waxed string. We were told that they were to be worn around the neck and should never be removed for any reason. We were told that there were two disks because if we should be killed in battle, the second disc would be removed and sent to Army records. It was a grim thought.

The following day we started doing physical training in the gymnasium. The instructors showed a sadistic disregard for us and picked on some individuals for no reason. One instructor yelled at one chap for having a dirty neck. 'Don't you use a mirror when you wash your neck?' he was asked. 'We don't have a hand mirror in our washroom, sergeant.' 'That's no excuse!' he howled back. 'Get one!' There was a stark contrast between the hot and cold washing facilities that the instructors enjoyed in their gym, and the cold water and cramped conditions in our washroom. (*Vere, 2006*) After this physical training session, we were marched to the armoury to draw our rifles and bayonets. All our drill from then on would be with a Lee-Enfield rifle on our shoulders.

In these first two weeks there were lectures in the mess hall on consecutive evenings. On the first evening, the lecture was given by the medical officer of the depot. He spoke to us about general health, hygiene and the perils of venereal disease. He told us that we had all been classified 'Grade One' and that it was up to us to stay that way!

The second lecture was delivered by the personnel selection officer. He told us about the process used to allocate individuals to certain roles. With a logic that I didn't quite follow, he went on to say, 'If you were a baker before you came here, we may find you better suited to become a driver, and so on.' He told us that not everyone could become a driver as there was a much greater need for infantrymen, but that we would all be given a series of intelligence tests shortly and the results would determine which of us would be trained as drivers. Although I had never driven any vehicle in my life, I decided there and then that this was the role for me. Who wants to be a PBI – a poor bloody infantryman?[23]

We then had our first lesson in fieldcraft. We were marched out to the training ground in the countryside. After a long march, we came to a place with fields, hedgerows, trees and muddy puddles all around. The corporal demonstrated how to crawl over the ground without leaving ourselves exposed to the enemy. Head well down, elbows fully extended, inching ourselves forward on our elbows and using our boots for that extra push.

The sergeant then made us stand in an extended line across the field and gave the order to drop to the ground and then wait for the order to advance over the field. He told us we must keep going regardless of whether there was mud or puddles in front of us. Just crawl through it and worry about cleaning ourselves up afterwards: 'Ad-vance!'

We started off over the wet and muddy ground, trying to keep a low profile as we moved forward. It proved to be slow and laborious work, needing a great deal of physical effort to move any great distance. After what seemed like an age, the sergeant called a halt, telling us to stand and look back at the distance we had covered. We were no more than 40m away from the start and some of the men were still way back down the course. We were all caked head to foot in thick, sticky mud that would take a lot of cleaning off later.

After a short break, the sergeant told us about how the Germans used their mortars. He told us that if a mortar shell lands in front of you, and then one lands behind, you know that they are range-finding and that the next ones will fall close by. He told us that when this happens the only option is to move out fast and take up another position. He said: 'It will help to keep your name off the village war memorial if you do.' I remembered these words later when I was dug in on Monte Camino. After the training session had ended, we were marched back to the barracks in the failing light of the winter afternoon, our uniforms stiff with the dried mud.

---

23 The term PBI. was first used in the *BEF Times*, 1 December 1916: 'So here's to the lads of the PBI Who live in a ditch that never is dry.'

Friday was pay day. With the company standing at ease, the colour sergeant called out the name of each man in alphabetical order. When called I jumped to attention and then advanced to a table where the officers were sitting. Halting in front of the table, I saluted and then signed my name on the form, while the officer recorded the amount I was to receive. The second officer then placed the money on the table in front of me – a grand total of 14 shillings.

Chapter 10

GENERAL SERVICE TRAINING

It was on a cold Monday morning in December 1942, that I progressed to general service training. On the first day, I was taught how to sight a rifle mounted on a tripod. This lesson took place on the perimeter of the parade ground with the targets on the far side. After each of us had had a go, the NCO pushed the rifle off target so as not to give the next man any advantage with his own sighting.

Drill continued to take up a third of the working day. The rest of the time was filled up with a mixture of lessons on the Bren gun, training with Mills hand grenades,[24] respirator training for gas attacks, long marches in battle order for toughening up, and obstacle courses.

The weapons training was led by a captain with a red face. We were marched to one of the many battle training areas outside the town. This one had high earthwork embankments with a brickwork enclosure. A tier of sandbags had been placed in front of the brickwork to protect the observers from any blast fragments.

The captain started his demonstration by blasting off a few rifle rounds into the sandbags. He then refilled the magazine of the rifle with ten rounds, which he fired in quick succession. Moving on to the Bren gun, he blasted away at the sandbags. He then picked up a Thompson submachine gun, which tore the jute sandbags apart with the impact from the heavy-calibre bullets. The last weapon was a very

24 'Mills bombs' were British hand grenades designed by William Mills and were the first modern fragmentation grenades used by the British Army. The Mills was a defensive grenade meant to be thrown from behind cover at a target in the open, wounding with fragmentation, as opposed to an offensive grenade, which does not fragment, relying on short-range blast effect to wound or stun the victim without endangering the thrower with fragments.

heavy Boys anti-tank rifle.[25] For this demonstration, the captain stuffed his ears with cotton wool. Lying down behind the rifle, he took aim and fired. The recoil of the Boys rifle was so powerful it pushed him back along the ground.

Having shown us the way to handle the various weapons, he then gave a demonstration on how to use a bayonet. Taking up his rifle, he fixed a bayonet into position and told us: 'When you bayonet your man, don't tickle him with it, stick the damn thing in like this.' He then launched himself at the straw-filled dummy, sticking his bayonet and half the rifle into it with the ferocity of his attack. Pulling the bayonet free, he turned round to us and snarled, 'After bayoneting and you can't remove the blade, what you must do is this.' Advancing once again to the dummy, he stabbed the bayonet into the straw chest and pulled the trigger: 'Blow the bugger off!'

We were all disgusted that the captain had made the awful act of bayoneting a man to death even more brutal. We talked about this man's lack of humanity long into the night, and I pondered if I would, soon, become equally brutalised when I saw active service. It was a sickening thought.

The following day we were taken to the indoor rifle range. There were four firing positions some 30m away from 10cm square targets. Each of the firing positions had a sandbag on the floor to enable each man to lie in a prone position with his rifle resting on the sandbag. The first four men took up their positions with the officer reminding us that he would be keeping score. He told us to hold our breath when squeezing the trigger and to try not to move our bodies, because this would move the rifle off the target. I fired: Crack, Crack, Crack … I think every shot of mine missed the targets!

The series of intelligence tests ran over several days and made a pleasant change. The first test was a simple multiple-choice paper. One question was based on two pictures showing trains having crashed on a bend in the track. One train had derailed on the inside of the bend, the other on the outside. The question posed was 'Which of the two pictures is correct?'

Another question showed two drawings of ships with steam billowing from their funnels. In one picture the steam went towards the bow of the ship and in the other the steam went towards the stern. We were required to draw an arrow to show which direction the ship

---

25 The Boys anti-tank rifle was a British anti-tank rifle used during the Second World War. It was often nicknamed the 'elephant gun' due to its size and large 14mm bore.

was heading. I found all the questions very easy, and I was confident that I had completed the test with a high score, if not full marks.

After a few days I was told that I was one of the few that would be offered the opportunity to be taught to drive, but before that I would need to complete two other parts of the training programme: a visit to the grenade range and a walk through the gas chamber, with and without a respirator on.

The visit to the grenade range was preceded by a lesson on arming the grenades. We had to unscrew the base plugs before priming them with the percussion cap with its seven-second fuse.[26] The sergeant explained that the grenade must be held in the throwing hand with the handle held down and with the safety pin in place. With the boxes of grenades now primed, the platoon marched out from the barracks, through the town and into the countryside. Because of petrol rationing, there was no traffic on the road, other than an occasional delivery van.

It was now mid-December 1942 with the leaves off the trees and the hedgerows looking bare and lifeless. The lanes were damp and silent, but the peace was broken by the sound of forty-three pairs of boots pounding the empty highway. We turned off the road and on to a track across a field with a large painted sign warning the public that it was War Department property and that this was a dangerous place.

In the field, there was a miniature fort made with sandbags in a wooden frame. At the front of the fort there was a throwing bay with high walls of sandbags on the sides and back, and a wall about 5ft high in the front. A passageway led back into the main part of the building with a 90-degree turn, to protect those inside from blast fragments should an accident occur in the throwing bay. The building had an observation platform, which was accessed via a wooden ladder.

The peace and quiet of the countryside was soon shattered by the blast of eighty bombs exploding at short intervals, sending their lethal pieces of shrapnel in all directions. The fort was hit repeatedly by fragments of grenades that fell short.[27] Having thrown all our grenades, we tidied up the blast fragments and marched back to the barracks in the gathering dusk.

---

26 The seven-second fuse was only used in training. The delay was reduced to four seconds in battle situations because in the Battle of France in 1940 the seven-second delay proved to be too long, giving defenders time to escape the explosion, or even to throw the grenade back.

27 A competent thrower could manage 15m with reasonable accuracy, but the grenade could throw lethal fragments about 91m.

A day or so later, our platoon was taken to the camp gas chamber. We were given a gas cape for overall protection, a respirator and an anti-gas wallet that held swabs and cream for use on infected skin. We were then marched to the gas chamber with our respirators in position on our chests and wearing our steel helmets. We arrived at a bleak building that had a door at each end with a long passage running from one end to the other.

The officer warned us that there was an element of danger in the process and that we must walk through the room with our respirators on, then do the same with them off. The intention was to replicate the conditions we could expect to encounter in a gas attack.

The corporal stood near the middle of the room next to a gas candle. The sergeant then put on his helmet and respirator and walked into the room to switch on a single light bulb. He then put a match to the candle and came out, closing both doors behind him. Removing his respirator, the sergeant told us that we must not try to hold our breath. If we did, he would force us to make a return trip!

Inside the room the light bulb provided only a dim glow in the moving fog of gas. The corporal, with his own respirator now on, took up his position in the room and we then walked in single file through the room. This was the easy part of the exercise. Once outside, the corporal told us to take off our respirators.

The first man started on his way through the passageway and after just a few steps, we could hear him gasping and coughing for breath as the first whiff of gas reached down into his lungs. We all followed through the door and suffered in the same way. The sergeant, who was still wearing his own respirator, helped those who needed it most through the doorway and into the fresh air. I was reasonably OK, but some members of the platoon were spluttering and being physically sick.

Later that afternoon, the sergeant took us for a run to clear away the traces of the gas we had in our systems. It was an effort to begin with, but the run helped to clear our lungs of the obnoxious gas, and I soon felt much better for it.

One evening we had an air raid drill, which required us to evacuate the entire barracks and move out to one of the training areas into a zigzag trench. After a few explosions in the distance, the 'all clear' sounded, enabling us to leave the bitterly cold and damp trench to return to our billets.

We entered the last week of our general service training at Christmas 1942. On Christmas morning, the platoon turned out to the main road that ran through the camp to hear the band playing a medley of popular tunes. Afterwards, the fife and drum section of the band marched up and down between the hundreds of men who had gathered to watch the display. It left us all feeling emotional and homesick.

For the Christmas dinner, an officer waited on us. Each man received a pint of beer and, as a concession, we were told that each billet could light up the fire to make it more comfortable. After our Christmas tea we settled round the fire and just talked. It was unlike any Christmas that I had experienced before. Oh, how I longed to be home in Drury Lane!

At reveille on Boxing Day morning, we were taken to the assault course and told that the company commander would accompany us on this exercise to recover from the excesses of the day before. We had little sympathy as none of us had had the chance to get a hangover. It was a very punishing course, and most of us struggled with the rope-over-the-water obstacle. A few of the men fell in with a mighty splash. By the time we had all completed the course we looked a sorry lot.

At the billet, we realised that this could very well be the last time we would be together because our new postings were due any day now. Although I had not made any lasting friendships, it was still rather sad that we were all going our separate ways. What would become of us? A random group of men who just happened to begin their war service on 13 November 1942.

The next morning, after the first parade and breakfast, the sergeant had us on the parade ground for drill for the last time. We were told that the personnel selection officer would inform us about our postings later that day. We all waited impatiently in the outer office to learn the decisions of the selection board. When it was my turn to go in, I saluted the officer sitting at his desk and gave him my name and number. He told me to sit down and said that I would be joining the Royal Berkshire Regiment as of 31 December. I would be staying on in the Meanee barracks but in new quarters. He told me that I had done quite well in the tests, and that I would be trained as a driver and would also join the Headquarters Company for a course on the mortar. He said: 'You know the kind of thing, like a length of drainpipe.' The course also included wireless procedure in the sending and receiving of messages. Then, with a serious look on his face he told me that if I failed the driving course or any other part of the course, I would be excluded from the mortars. He asked me if I had any questions and then wished me good luck.

Later, when everyone had seen the selection officer, I found there were only two other members of my platoon who would be joining me in the driver training, while the other men would leave the barracks to join their new battalions for infantry training. That evening, the platoon officer came into our billet to wish us well in our new postings. After having said goodbye to my friends of the last six weeks, I left the billet for the last time.

Chapter 11

DRIVING LESSONS

On New Year's Day, I made my way with my kit to the new quarters, just 150m away from my first billet. My new quarters were in one of several single-storey buildings that housed the mortar, signals and carrier platoons. The men in the mortar hut were in various stages of their training, with some about to finish and new men arriving at two-weekly intervals. This building had the luxury of hot and cold running water and a wireless set.

One of our first duties was to listen to a lecture from our new company commander, who told us not to run away with any grand ideas about ourselves because we had done well in the intelligence tests. He reminded us that if we messed up any part of the training, at any stage, we would be returned to the rifle groups. He then broke the news that none of us would be eligible for any kind of leave until the end of the course. Not even a twenty-four-hour pass would be issued until the training was completed because 'the war effort must take priority over all other considerations'. (*Vere, 2006*)

No leave! We had sixteen more weeks of training in front of us. We were all furious. It seemed so unjust having to serve over five months without returning home, but after much grumbling we settled down again and time passed fast enough.

The training was much of the same as that already covered in our first six weeks, but the fieldcraft was more arduous, and we came back most nights covered in wet mud that had to be removed by first parade the next day.

When we finally completed our infantry training, we started on the mortar course. For the next fourteen weeks, we were expected to master this apparently simple but quite complex piece of weaponry. The introductory talk was given by the platoon sergeant. He told us that we would be training on the mortar from Monday to Thursday and that we would undergo driving instruction on the roads on Friday mornings, with the Friday afternoons spent on driving on the rough country training ground. We were then allocated to groups of three, which made up a mortar gun crew. Each group was allocated an instructor who would take us through the mortar drill.

On the first day of our training, the corporal marched us to the mortar stores, where each crew was given a 3in mortar and a harness for transporting the gun. The mortar gun is a lot heavier than it looks and lifting it required physical strength as each part weighed around 18kg. The harness was designed to be worn over the right shoulder on extended marches. However, it was uncomfortable to wear as it cut deep into your shoulder.

The training began with a demonstration by an experienced mortar gun crew. The three pieces of the mortar gun were laid out on the ground in front of the men about ten paces from where they stood at ease. At the command of 'Attention', the crew sprang into position waiting for the next command of 'Action', at which they ran forward and threw themselves on to the ground behind their piece of gun. There, lying dead still, they waited for the next command of 'Action', at which they leapt to their feet, snatching the pieces of the gun from the ground, and ran forward to the mounting position where the mortar gun was assembled. The 'Number One' member of the crew then called out: 'Ready to fire!' After that they dismantled the mortar gun and ran back with the three parts to their former positions, where they stood to attention.

The corporal then marched us out of the barracks to one of the training sites for our first lesson. He then demonstrated the correct way to assemble the three parts of the mortar gun. Calling for three volunteers to step forward, the corporal walked about 7m in front of us and pushed an aiming post into the ground with the heel of his boot. The aiming post had a hinged bar at the base and one in the centre so that it could be folded together when not in use. It was painted with black and white bands and a diamond-shaped aiming point at the top.

The corporal told us that we would be repeating this drill many hundreds of times over the next fourteen weeks, and that later in the training we would be timed with a stopwatch to measure our speed and progress. He then picked up the baseplate of the gun and placed it on the ground, pointing in the general direction of the aiming post. He then moved it around on its cast iron spikes until he was sure that the barrel recess and sides of the plate were of equal portions to the post.

Next, he lifted and placed the barrel into the socket of the plate, giving it a quarter turn, locking it into position to keep it secure when fired.

He kept up a running commentary while he did all this and explained that the base plug held the firing pin at its centre and fired the bomb automatically when contact was made. With help from one of the men, he removed the leather barrel cover and unhooked the retention spring on its side. Now with the legs of the bipod standing fully extended and locked in position, it was placed over the muzzle and slipped down the barrel to its retaining collar. The retention spring held the mortar parts firmly together.

The corporal now returned the cover to the barrel. He then removed the gunsight from its protective case and put it carefully in place and locked it in position, During this procedure the corporal explained that it would often be necessary to adjust the angle of the barrel, particularly if the mortar was mounted on uneven ground. The process involved the Number Three placing his hand on the barrel while he turned a handle before relocking the clamp.

The corporal went on to explain that every time you dismantled the mortar, the first thing to do was to unlock the gunsight, set it back to zero, and then return it to the box. The next step was to return the yoke to the centre position while Number Two removed the retaining spring from the yoke.

After a pause, he explained that Number Two must now wait for Number Three to wind down the vertical range handle to the bottom. Once he had done this, Number Three slipped the yoke from the top of the barrel while Number Two returned the spring to the barrel and removed it from the baseplate by giving it the quarter turn. Having finished his rundown of the dismantling sequence, the corporal turned to us and asked, 'Any questions?'

We all stayed silent. My mind was spinning. I thought to myself that I would never remember all this, but I said nothing. I could see from the faces of the other men that we were all thinking the same.

After the demonstration, the corporal called the first three-man crew forward and ordered them to repeat the drill. They made a decent enough attempt at the beginning, but they struggled with the parts and got in each other's way. After a few moments it was clear that they had lost the thread of the assembly order.

The next crew was called forward and they did a little better before also coming unstuck. However, as each crew had a go, they became progressively better as the process began to sink in as they learned from the mistakes of the others.

At the end of the day, the corporal marched us back from the cold training ground for our tea, and back at our billet we talked over our first day of mortar training with some of the men who were more advanced. One thing they all agreed on was that the mortar course was no picnic. The assembly and dismantling process was complicated enough, but it required a great deal of stamina to carry the mortar for long distances. I was glad that I was strong enough to be able to cope with this. Some of the platoon, even after their eight weeks of physical training, had found it too much for them and had dropped out. I thought back to the personnel selection officer who had described the 3in mortar as a 'length of drainpipe'. I don't think he had ever lifted a mortar gun in his life!

For most of that first week, the training focused on getting us familiar with the first stage of just mounting the mortar. In the second week, we changed over to the full mortar mounting drill using the routine that had been demonstrated to us on the first day of our training, including dismantling the gun.

The corporal said that we might be wondering why we were being asked to repeat the same drill time after time, but he explained that this wasn't just to waste time but to enforce discipline. It seemed to me that most of what we were taught was designed to make us act like killing machines rather than human beings. It was much like the drill each morning on the barrack square, day in day out. What purpose did it serve? The Army didn't want us to think. It wanted us to obey orders and to kill and maim our fellow men without compunction.

I guess the corporal sensed that I was getting tired of all this, and he turned to me and said: 'There is a real point to this, you know. One day you might well find that the speed at which you get in and out of action will be important to your own survival.' This seemed a reasonable point and so I knuckled down to the drill and made up my mind that our crew would be the fastest in the whole platoon. After more drill, we had a peaceful evening in the billet, and that enabled me to write letters home to my mother and my sister, Nora.

The next day, it was straight back into the same mortar routine. Every crew had to repeat this routine three times, with each crew member changing their role after each circuit. The first full parade of the day was held outside Company HQ Office, on a small parade ground tucked away from the main camp. One reason for this muster was to count the men on parade and call the roll. The entire Headquarters Company was formed up into three sides of a square by platoon with the Company Sergeant Major (CSM) calling the roll and the captain strolling up and down looking at his men.

Having counted us all, the CSM called the parade to 'Attention' and marched towards the company commander with a good deal of foot stamping. Halting in front of the captain, he gave the salute 'Present and correct, sir!' The captain returned the salute with a wave of his hand before addressing us. He told us that those men who were finishing the course this week would undergo firing with live ammunition on the mortar range. The new intake would accompany them, primarily to guard the perimeter of the range during the firing, but also to let us see the mortar fired at close hand. After being dismissed we all turned to our right and saluted the captain.

On the day of the mortar shoot, we were briefed that our main responsibility was to keep civilians away from the danger zone. There were several footpaths in the area, which were marked by large red warning flags. We were told to wear our steel helmets and not to wander away from our guard positions.

We were transported to the firing range in a Bedford truck. The men who were going to do the firing were already waiting with the parts of the mortar guns strapped in position at the rear. Behind the lorry was a Bren gun carrier bearing high-explosive mortar bombs in cases of three.

After waiting on the lorry for fifteen minutes or so, the captain emerged from the office, strolled over and got in the cab. We were then on our way, with the Bren gun carriers bringing up the rear and making a terrific noise on the tarmac road surface. We drove for several miles before we arrived at the 'live' firing range.

Our group stood at the back, looking on as a mortar was set up very carefully by the platoon sergeant. Once he was satisfied with the set-up, we could see that the aiming post and mortar were lined up on some large wooden barrels about 700m away. The mortar bombs fired there previously had left the landscape barren and scarred.

We were taken round to our guard positions. Two men were dropped off at every point on the footpath, each of which were marked by a large red flag. The NCO warned us not to leave our spot. When the firing started, I was surprised that the mortar shell made a thump rather than a loud bang. You could just about pick up the flight of the bomb in the air, flying up in a high arc before falling to earth, slowly at first then speeding up until the explosion occurred.

After some minutes, we heard the thump of another mortar being fired and knew that a second mortar bomb was on its way. This one fell not too far from us, and we were taken by surprise by the detonation of its charge of high explosive and the complete disintegration of the shell. It sent lethal fragments of shrapnel over a wide area, making the most vicious whining sounds in the process.

We then heard all the mortars being fired together and the succession of distant thumps. These noises were soon surpassed by the explosions of the bombs falling to earth. They seemed to be getting closer and closer to our position. In fact, they were so close that my mate and I laid down on the pathway and buried our faces in the tufts of coarse grass at the edge of the track. While still in that position, a piece of shrapnel zipped into the grass landing no more than a few paces from our faces.

When the shelling stopped, I reached out and picked up the bright lump of steel with its jagged edges. It was still warm. I took one look at this deadly piece of deformed metal and thought about its wider implications for us in the future. I passed it to my mate, who told me, 'I'm going to get this mounted so I can wear it on my watch chain!' Some people are strange. I couldn't understand why anyone would want to carry round a piece of metal that could have killed us!

The following day we were given instruction in the gunsight. The corporal had drawn one sight for each three-man crew from the storeman, who acted as if he was giving away his babies rather than War Department kit. We had, of course, already seen the sight during the demonstrations, but we had never been able to examine it in detail and at first-hand.

The mortar gunsight was made entirely of brass. One of its key features was a curved sliding scale marked off in increments of 25 yards (equivalent to 22m). There were two separate scales with a pointer. The first pointer was for 'charge one' and the second for 'charge two'. The two options were based on the amount of propellent charge used for each bomb. For 'charge one' you were required to remove half of the propellant charge from the bomb, so that 'charge one' was set for the 'minimum range'. 'Charge two', which was set with the full amount of propellent charge, was set for the 'maximum range' of around 1.6km.

The moving scale was locked into position by a large wing nut on the right-hand side of the sight. At the top of the sight was a small optical device. This held a triangle with a translucent background mounted in a metal tube. This was only used when night aiming was required, when the aiming lamp was fixed on to the foremost of the two aiming posts. The open gunsight was fixed by the side of the tube and consisted of two sturdy metal triangles about 4cm apart that were used for general sighting of the gun.

The corporal carried on talking all through the demonstration, trying to explain the intricate parts of the sight and their technical terms and functions. He moved on to describe the turret head. This was the part of the mortar that carried the two aiming sights. This was fixed, but you could move the optical night aiming sight by means of an adjustable screw. This enabled it to be lined up with the aiming lamp on the far post. The turret head could be made to rotate by means of two knurled knobs, one either side of it and linked together by a concealed worm drive. These knobs drove a gearwheel fastened to the centre of the turret. On the base of the turret there were engraved calibrations in degrees and half-degrees. Facing the turret, the Number One would find the 'Degrees Left' on the right side, and the 'Degrees Right' on the left side. This seemed back to front, but the corporal explained that if you had the mortar mounted and zeroed on the aiming post, and you receive a command of, say, 'Left 50 degrees, 30 minutes', Number One would first move the turret from its zero position by twisting the knurled knob to the position where the reading on the turret of 'Left 50 degrees, 30 minutes' corresponded with zero on the base. The corporal explained that by moving it left, the sight had moved right of the aiming post. Finally, it was all starting to make a little more sense.

The corporal continued pumping out information, knowing full well that some of his group had almost lost touch with him at times. He carried on explaining that having manually moved the mortar to the left, the two bubbles in the spirit level were no longer in their central positions. To address this, Number One and Number Two had to turn the handles of the vertical range and the longitudinal range. This set both bubbles moving, so Number One and Number Two had to talk to each other to confirm when their bubble was central. After all this, Number One had to make sure that the aiming triangle was still looking at the aiming post.

To ask a question would only have complicated things in our heads, so we all remained silent. Sensing our discomfort, the corporal suggested that it would be a good idea to write this all down in a notebook to help us when we were in our examination after the course had finished. A few of us went into town looking for a stationer that afternoon.

We were still required to attend physical training sessions in the gym twice a week. I hated these sessions. In fact, I don't think any of my mates in the platoon liked the instructors very much with their overbearing sense of physical superiority. They seemed to take great pleasure in inflicting misery on anyone who was even slightly overweight and not in peak condition. I made up my mind that one day soon, I would get my own back on one instructor who struck me as a sadistic bully who should probably have been in prison rather than the Army.

Friday 15 January was to be the day of our first driving lesson. We were told to wear our greatcoats and steel helmets. It had been made clear to us that every member of the mortar crew was expected to be able to drive a Bren gun carrier and this was therefore a central element of the training. We were all rather apprehensive at the thought of driving a vehicle for the first time, and I was very aware that it might well be a once-only event if I failed to pick up the basics of driving as that would mean being kicked off the course.

For my driver training, I was allocated to a team of five trainees under a corporal driving instructor. We were allocated to a Fordson truck that had undoubtedly seen better days, having been wrecked at the hands of hundreds of would-be drivers. I soon discovered that our driving instructor had a dry sense of humour (and, my goodness, he needed one!).

It was on our third day out that I got my first chance to drive. Climbing into the driving seat, the instructor reminded me to change gears when we came to bends in the road. The Fordson truck had a crash gearbox; that is a mesh gearbox that required some very specific driving skills when going up and down hills. On the way up, the 'engine side' gears used to spin faster than needed, so the driver just needed to wait until they were turning at roughly the same speed as the 'roadside'. On the way down, the manoeuvre was more complex. First, the clutch had to be depressed, and then the gear lever moved into neutral. Second, the clutch had to be released at the same time as the throttle was touched to speed up the 'engine side' gears. The driver then had to depress the clutch again, and, at just the right moment, slip the lever into the lower gear.

I was driving quite happily on the flat with the corporal in the passenger seat and four other trainees sat in the back of the truck. Although the snow was packed hard on the road, all was going well until we came over the brow of a hill. I tried to change down but found that I could not get the lorry back in gear.

With the truck picking up speed I looked at the corporal, who was hanging on to the roll bars with a mad grin on his face. This made me panic and so I stood on the brake pedal. That soon wiped the look off his face. The truck started to waltz round and round down the hill. I had lost control and nearly hit a lamppost at the bottom of the hill. The corporal shouted at me: 'You nearly killed us all. If you did this in a Churchill tank, you'd have demolished the effin' village.' He and I looked behind us. The back of the truck was empty. My four mates having jumped out as the lorry had careered down the hill!

The following week I had the chance to try again, and I did much better this time. By week three I was beginning to feel like a competent driver. It was then that I was told that in the following week, I would be trained to drive a Bren gun carrier.

When the big day arrived, we were marched to the motor pool that was tucked away in a corner of the camp and we were allocated in groups of four to three Bren gun carriers. Unfortunately, the weather was foul and with its open top and sides exposed to the elements, the carrier was not the best form of transport in wet weather.

Our instructor was a large man, and he let us know from the beginning that he was in charge. Having driven us out of town, he pulled up at the foot of a hill that ran out into the countryside. He turned and asked us if we had ever driven before we had joined the Army. When we all said 'no', he told me to come forward into the driving seat of the Bren gun carrier. I had already decided beforehand that I would take the risk of making a fool of myself and so I willingly squeezed myself in under the steering wheel, which was only centimetres from my chest. The sergeant then gave us a general rundown on the procedure to be followed when driving this type of vehicle.

One noticeable difference to the lorry was the gear-changing lever, which was slotted into a brass plate. The slots were in the shape of the letter 'H' and numbered at each corner, giving the gear position from 1 to 4 (with a cutout for 'REV' for reverse). I found the brass plate certainly helped me find the correct gear when compared to the slack box of tricks that served as a gearbox on the Fordson lorry.

Starting off on the slope of the hill with the engine running and the foot and handbrake off, I found that by imposing a slight lock on the steering wheel, I could slow the speed of the carrier and prevent it from running away downhill. The sergeant guided me through accelerating to give the engine more power, before changing into second and then third gear. On that first lesson I never made it up to top gear – the thing weighed over 7,000kg!

Most of the men did well that morning, and we all felt pleased with ourselves when we went off for our midday meal, looking forward to the afternoon and our cross-country driving. For the afternoon session we had a different instructor, a middle-aged lance corporal. He was not a young man, but he was an excellent driving instructor, and his hints and advice were helpful. The training ground used by the carriers was in light woodlands criss-crossed by many footpaths, some of which were deeply rutted by carrier tracks. These ruts were very deep in places and once or twice left the carrier grounded on its hull. The instructor told us that on one occasion a Bren gun carrier had rolled over and the occupants inside were all crushed. Because of this risk it was an Army regulation that only the NCO and the man undergoing the driving lesson were allowed on board during this cross-country training.

Driving over the uneven paths was like a ride on a fairground ride and at any other time might have been quite enjoyable if it were not for the fear of toppling over. The instructor pointed out one feature in the training ground where there was a very deep and wide hole, flat at the bottom but with very steep sides all round. He told me that I would have to become a lot more proficient before I would be allowed to try that.

The following Friday, we were told that now we had mastered the basics we would be taken out on a longer run under the supervision of the senior sergeant of the motor pool. The route was a new concrete road made not long before the start of the war that ran from Colchester to Clacton-on-Sea, a journey of 24km. As we left Colchester, we found that we had the road to ourselves, and we stopped several times so that each of us could take a turn behind the wheel.

After we had gone about 10km, the instructor stopped us and had us practising backing up the carrier down a lane. This was not an easy task. To see where you were going, the driver had to stand at the wheel and turn his head and body round until he could see over the top of the engine cover. This wasn't an easy manoeuvre, as we all found out, particularly for those who were big around the middle.

The senior sergeant told us that he knew a café along the seafront in Clacton where we could get a nice cup of tea and a cheese sandwich. As we approached the town, we heard several very loud explosions up ahead, even above the noise of the engine and the carrier tracks on the road.

We drove on through the town centre and came out on to the seafront. I gazed in wonder at my first sight of the sea since that trip to Hastings with my father some ten or more years ago. The smell of the salty air, the wide expanse of the sea and the curvature of the horizon left me exhilarated. I had almost forgotten that such sublime beauty still existed in this world. It was a wonderful sight.

This moment of peaceful reverie was soon shattered by the blast of a series of very loud explosions. This was the noise that we had heard when we were outside the town. The source of the noise was a row of three Bofors guns[28] deployed on the shingle beach some 30m back

28 The Bofors 40mm Automatic Gun L/60 was an anti-aircraft cannon, designed in the 1930s by the Swedish arms manufacturer AB Bofors. The gun was designed as an intermediate anti-aircraft gun. It was used by eighteen countries in the Second World War, including most of the Allies and Nazi Germany and Hungary.

from the high-water mark. They were blazing away at a windsock that was being towed offshore behind a light aircraft. The noise of the guns was deafening.

Having reached the café on the seafront, the sergeant climbed out of his carrier and went inside. We all piled in behind him. The sergeant was right about the quality of the food. The bread and cheese were wonderful and so was the large mug of hot sweet tea. It was just what we needed after our cold journey. None of us asked where the extra rations had come from. We were simply happy to have found the place.

On the way back from Clacton we each took a turn at the wheel, and we arrived back at the camp in time for our midday meal. For the first time since we joined the Army, we weren't particularly hungry.

The afternoon session was spent driving the Bren gun carrier in the mud of the wood and thickets, churning up the ground whenever we moved off the tracks. The moving parts of the Bren gun carrier, such as the sprockets, bogie and tracks soon got encased in mud. I never figured out why, but we were never asked to clean the carriers no matter how dirty they became. Someone must have had the job of cleaning them as the Bren gun carriers were always clean when we took them back on the road.

The weeks were flying by now and we moved on to learn the wireless procedure. The training was led by a sergeant from the signal platoon and involved the sending and receiving of messages on two types of radio set: the Wireless Set 17 and Wireless Set 22.

The Wireless Set 17 set was a portable transceiver that was used as a ground station for communication between detachments. It had a range of around 25km. This set was quite bulky and was designed primarily for use in the carrier (although it could be carried in a 'man-pack' if needed). The sergeant showed us how to net two sets together on the same frequency, enabling messages to be passed between them.

We learned that all conversations over the airwaves had to be carried out using the correct wireless procedure and the phonetic alphabet: Alpha, Bravo, Charlie and so on. This involved keeping the messages short and simple, and avoiding saying anything inappropriate because all conversations were monitored by (female) operators. He warned us: 'Watch what you say.'

We then moved on to lessons on 3in mortar ammunition. The corporal explained to us that when in the stores six bombs were kept together in a strong container. However, on active service three bombs were carried in a portable waterproof container weighing around 13kg.

He then took one of the bombs out of the container of three. It was around 30cm long with its aluminium safety cap. He explained that the safety cap was not unscrewed until the time of firing. This cap protected another thin metal cap that sat over the detonator, which reacted instantaneously on impact with the high explosive in the bomb. When the bomb fell down the barrel of the mortar, the velocity of the shell would cause a steel ball and spring mechanism inside the detonator to drop into place so that it could not return to its former position. This action left the bomb armed.

The bomb had a raised band on the top called the 'tolerance band' or 'driving band', which made sure that the bomb fitted snugly into the barrel, but without being too tight. At the tail of the bomb, there was a waterproof cover that was attached to the top of the fins with a tape. The tape was wrapped around the fins and was tied with a bow so it could be removed without any fuss when it was about to be fired. At the bottom of the cover, there was also a cupped steel base to stop any accidental firing of the cartridge if the round was dropped or mishandled in any way.

The corporal reminded us that the firing pin at the bottom of the barrel came into use when the bomb was dropped down the barrel. The force of the falling bomb would hit the pin that automatically discharges the cartridge into the propellant charge.[29] The charge was in capsules set out around the tailfins and held in position by close-wound springs. The fins were attached to the bomb in pairs and spot-welded to withstand the blast as the bomb is sent on its way and to prevent the bomb from becoming unstable. The corporal ended there with, 'Come on. Let's get some tea. There will be more for tomorrow.'

As he promised, there was more of this on the next day. The corporal repeated much of the information from the previous day but then told us he would teach us about where we might expect the bomb to land if fired at a target. He explained that when the mortar was fired on 'charge one', three of the capsules of propellent were removed from around the tailfins. As a result, the bomb would travel a shorter distance. When the mortar was fired on 'charge two', six capsules of propellent were placed in the tailfins, giving the mortar its range of 1.6km. This, however, made the bomb less accurate.

The corporal explained that the place where the bombs were supposed to land was called the 'beaten zone', and the actual place that it landed depended on several factors. The crew might set the mortar sight incorrectly or fail to centralise the bubbles in the spirit levels. In addition, things like wear in the barrel, slight variations in the propellant charge, and weather conditions might all affect the

29 The propellent was nitrocellulose yellow.

flight of the bomb. With the mortar's rapid rate of fire, the aim was to concentrate as much fire as practicable on and around the target; the thinking being that even if the bombs missed the target, they would still cause anxiety and confusion on the ground.

The next day, we were taken out into the countryside in Bren gun carriers, carrying the mortars, dummy ammunition cases and picks and shovels. On arrival at our destination, the corporal gathered us around him and told us that we were going to dig some trenches capable of holding the three crew members, the mortar and ammunition. The trench needed to be big enough to allow room for the crew to work in. He told us that every time we confronted the enemy on the battlefield, we would be expected to dig such a trench. Ideally, the trench would be dug secretly at night and in a more exposed position than would be possible during daylight hours. The aim was to have the mortar mounted and ready to fire before the trench was completed. The corporal stressed that it was in everyone's interest to get below ground level as soon as possible, leaving just the leather muzzle cover of the mortar visible above ground.

As no more than two men could work on the trench at any one time, the third member of the crew was required to dig three individual slit trenches, each capable of accommodating one man. Having dug out the trenches, he then told us to mount our mortar, making sure that it was on firm ground on the floor of the trench. When the mortar was ready, he took a pick and made a line with the pointed end about 15cm in front of the bipod's feet and told us to take up our correct positions at the gun in the trench. He made sure that 'Number One' had enough space to crouch down. He then made a line at right angles, giving 'Number Two' and 'Number Three' enough room to place the ammunition cases.

The next day we continued our training on communications with the signal sergeant. Gradually we became more proficient with the portable wireless sets, and we were introduced to the self-powering field telephone. This was designed to enable a detachment commander to communicate via a length of cable back to the mortar position and the 'Number One' crew member. The microphone was strapped around the neck and throat and the power was induced by speaking into the throat microphone, which generated electrical impulses that could be picked up in the earpieces at the other end. This form of microphone gave 'Number One' the freedom of both hands to adjust the mortar without having to hold the telephone in his hand.

We were now due some leave, having completed sixteen weeks of training and having had no leave of absence in almost six months.

Before we were released, we had the agony of the wait for our exam and test results. To my great relief, I passed both the mortar tests and my driving tests in the highest level for track-laying vehicles and given Army Form A.2038. I went off on leave with a spring in my step and, do you know, that was the only driving test that I ever took!

I enjoyed my time back home with my family, but it soon passed as I couldn't shake off the foreboding that, upon return from our leave, I would be sent overseas to war. Too soon I found myself on the train back to Colchester.

Chapter 12

BRITAIN AND THE USA JOIN FORCES

A great deal had happened while I was going through my training. Churchill had got his way and planning for the second front in Italy had begun. To this day it frustrates me. I have this vision of Churchill, lounging in his padded silk dressing gown at Chequers and Chartwell, dreaming of easy victories and the eternal gratitude of the British people. What thought did he give to the likely human cost of the victory that he imagined? Had he ever studied a map of Italy? Did he know nothing about the Italian climate in winter?

The libraries are full of eulogies to Churchill, but one of the most authentic, first-hand appraisals of Churchill is contained in Brooke's war diaries. Brooke was often overly critical of the man, and in one particularly telling passage he hit the nail on the head:

> He knows no details, has only got half the picture in his mind, talks absurdities and it makes my blood boil to listen to his nonsense. I find it hard to remain civil. And the wonderful thing is that half of the population of the world imagine that Winston Churchill is one of the Strategists of History, a second Marlborough, and the other half have no conception what a public menace he is and has been throughout this war! It is far better that the world should never know, and never suspect the feet of clay of that otherwise superhuman being. (*Brooke, 1957*)

Lord Moran, Churchill's personal physician, recognised that Brooke's comments would be unpopular because they challenged the Churchill myth. He wrote:

> There was a feeling of dismay when the [Alanbrook] Diaries were published that the [Churchill] legend had been scratched. Nobody, it appeared, wanted to argue about Winston's skill or lack of skill in planning the strategy of the war, though that is the crucial issue raised by the Diaries. Nobody was prepared to see him treated dispassionately as an historical figure. People disliked the Diaries because they loved Winston. (*Moran, 1966*)

And there lies one of the primary faults in the British war effort. None of those who were able to influence Churchill ever felt able to question or challenge his judgement. They knew that he never listened.

In January 1943, Churchill and Roosevelt met again, at Casablanca this time, to deal with the implications of their previous strategic decisions. The conference resulted in an announcement that the Allies would accept nothing less than the unconditional surrender of the Axis powers. In a radio broadcast to the American people, Roosevelt explained what he meant by unconditional surrender: 'We mean no harm to the common people of the Axis nations. But we do mean to impose punishment and retribution upon their guilty, barbaric leaders.' (*Roosevelt F.D., 1943*)

Roosevelt made the announcement to keep Soviet forces engaged with Germany on the Eastern Front, and to prevent Stalin from negotiating a separate peace with the Nazi regime. Throughout the conference, Roosevelt's attention was focused primarily on the Pacific War front and he regarded the Italian strategy as a sop to maintain good relations with Churchill. Having examined the plans drawn up by his generals, Roosevelt was forced to conclude that the Allies simply did not have enough men, ships or supplies to fight in the Pacific, the Mediterranean and across the English Channel.

The conduct of the negotiations at Casablanca further confirmed Churchill's reputation for stubborn, pig-headed cunning in the eyes of the American generals. Before the conference, Roosevelt had warned that the British would come with a plan and stick to it and he was right. Once again, the Americans arrived with disagreements among themselves while the British turned up armed with a host of statistics and logistical projections. Churchill stressed that an invasion of Italy provided a suitable alternative to a cross-Channel invasion and that an Italian campaign would be short but would accelerate the ending of the war. To address American concerns that Allied forces might get bogged down in Italy he (reputedly) told Roosevelt: 'Britain's prime and capital foe is not Italy, but Germany, the strategic concept is to make the former a "springboard, not a sofa".'[30]

Upset at being railroaded by Churchill and Roosevelt, Wedemeyer cabled back to Washington: 'The British descended on me like locusts ... We came, we saw, we were conquered.' (*Reynolds, 1988*)

Churchill's strategy, such as it was, was to force the Germans to commit the maximum number of divisions in Italy. He argued that this would create the time needed for the Allies to prepare for a cross-Channel invasion.

The British Chiefs of Staff proposed that the campaign should begin with an invasion of Sardinia, arguing that it would force Germany to disperse its forces. The Americans thought the plan was opportunistic and irrelevant, but they were persuaded by Churchill to agree to an invasion of Sicily on the grounds of the savings to Allied shipping that would result from the removal of Axis air and naval forces from the island. However, Brooke was far from happy with Churchill's fickle decision-making. He wrote:

> [Churchill] loved these sudden changes of plans. Unfortunately, he often wished to carry out similar sudden changes in strategy! I had the greatest difficulty in making him realise that strategy was a long-term process in which you could not frequently change your mind. He did not like being reminded of this fact and frequently shook his fist in my face and said, 'I do not want any of your long-term projects, all they do is cripple initiative.' (*Brooke, 1957*)

30 Whether Churchill actually used these words is open to question. Although it is attributed to Churchill in numerous biographies, the words appear to have been first used in the play *Soldiers; an obituary for Geneva*, written by Rolf Hochhuth in 1968.

Chapter 13

INVASION OF SICILY

The plans for the invasion of Sicily were drawn up by General Bernard Montgomery. He identified that there were four good ports with the necessary capacity to support an invasion fleet: Messina, Catania, Syracuse and Palermo. Messina was heavily guarded by fixed defences and beyond the range of Allied fighter aircraft, and Catania was also heavily defended. Syracuse and Palermo on the other hand were both within Allied fighter cover and not so heavily defended.

The outline plan that was presented to Eisenhower involved dispersed landings by large numbers of Allied troops in the south-east, south and north-west areas of Sicily with the aim of capturing Catania, Palermo, Syracuse, Licata and Augusta, before moving on to take Messina. The logic behind the plan was that it would result in the rapid capture of key Axis airfields and the capture of all the main ports on the island. This would facilitate a build-up of Allied troops, as well as denying their use to the Axis forces.

Detailed planning for the operation was inhibited by the fact that the three commanders – Alexander, Montgomery, and Patton – were fully occupied in operations in Tunisia. It was not until 2 May that Montgomery met Eisenhower and convinced him to concentrate the Allied effort on the south-east corner of Sicily. Not for the last time, Montgomery's arguments made sense, but his manner irritated the Americans with his conceit and overpowering belief in his own superiority.

On 17 May, Alexander defined the tasks of the two armies. He intended to establish Allied forces along a line from Catania to Licata. He later wrote that at that stage it was not practicable to plan further ahead but that his intentions were clear: he intended to drive north to Santo Stefano on the northern coast to split the island in two and cut the Axis armies' east–west communications. The American 7th Army was assigned to land in the Gulf of Gela, in south-central Sicily, to establish a beachhead stretching over 50km. The British 8th Army was assigned to land in south-eastern Sicily. Their beach front also stretched 40km, leaving a gap of some 40km between the two Armies.

Once the Axis forces had been defeated in Tunisia, the Allied strategic bomber force commenced attacks on the main principal airfields of Sardinia, Sicily and southern Italy, and the ports of Naples, Messina, Palermo and Cagliari. The attacks were spread to maintain uncertainty as to the next Allied move, and to pin down Axis aircraft and keep them away from Sicily. Bombing of northern Italy (by aircraft based in the UK) and Greece (by aircraft based in the Middle East) was increased. Beach defences were left alone, to preserve surprise as to where the landings would occur.

A naval bombardment and seaborne landing by British troops on 11 June (*Operation Corkscrew*) secured the Pelagie Islands of Lampedusa and Linosa, some 140km west of Malta.

To distract the Axis forces, the Allies engaged in several deception operations. The most famous and successful of these was *Operation Mincemeat*. This was conceived by Naval intelligence officer Ewen Montagu and RAF Squadron Leader Charles Cholmondeley.

A corpse, dressed in the uniform of a Royal Marines officer and carrying fake documents, was allowed to drift ashore in Spain. The documents purported to reveal that the Allies were planning an invasion of Greece. German intelligence accepted the authenticity of the documents, and the Germans diverted much of their defensive effort from Sicily to Greece. The Germans also transferred a group of minesweepers and minelayers from Sicily and laid three additional minefields off the Greek coast.

By 10 July, only two airfields in Sicily remained fully operational and over half the Axis aircraft had been forced to leave the island. Over the ten-week period of air attacks, Allied airman flew 42,227 sorties and destroyed 323 German and 105 Italian aircraft, for the loss of 250 aircraft, mostly to anti-aircraft fire over Sicily.

The plan was settled that the invasion of Italy (code-named *Operation Husky*) would begin with an amphibious assault of Sicily by two Allied armies, one landing on the south-eastern and one on the central southern coast. The Allied land forces were drawn from the American, British and Canadian armies, and were structured as two task forces. The British 8th Army under Montgomery's command landed on the south-east corner of the Island. The American 7th Army, under General George S. Patton Jr, landed on Montgomery's left with the task of protecting his left flank to enable Montgomery to drive up the east coast through Catania to the Strait of Messina.

The amphibious assaults were to be supported by naval gunfire, as well as tactical bombing, and close air support by the combined air forces. As such, the operation required a complex command structure. Eisenhower, as Commander-in-Chief of all the Allied forces in North Africa, was the overall commander, with Harold Alexander acting as his second-in-command. The overall Naval Force Commander was Admiral Sir Andrew Cunningham.

The American commanders were resentful about being relegated to a secondary role in the campaign and thought that their value had been underestimated. It was certainly true that Montgomery had doubts about the ability of Americans, who had suffered some embarrassing defeats in their first encounters with the Germans in Africa. To his mind the British 8th Army had been tested and proven in North Africa and was entitled to play a dominant role in the coming campaign.

The invasion involved 3,300 ships and seven Allied divisions (which was two more than were deployed on D-Day). It is, to this day, the largest amphibious operation in history. On observing the armada, an American war correspondent wrote: 'There is no way of conveying the enormous size of that fleet. On the horizon it resembled a distant city. It covered half the skyline ... Even to be part of it was frightening. I hope no American ever has to see its counterpart sailing against us.' (*St Louis Post-Dispatch,* 1943)

In addition to the amphibious landings, airborne troops were flown in to support both task forces. The pilots and navigators of these transport aircraft were mostly Americans, and they had not been adequately trained. The aircraft ran into high winds shortly after take-off and their V-formations broke up before they reached Sicily. The 3,400 American paratroopers were scattered all over the south-east of the island.

The British troops who were carried in gliders fared even worse. A total of 129 American Waco gliders and eight British Horsas were towed by 109 American Dakotas, seven RAF Halifax bombers and twenty-one RAF Armstrong Whitworth Albemarles. Their target was a landing zone west of the Maddalena peninsula. The aircraft and gliders took off from Kairouan in Tunisia and followed a complex route to avoid being picked up by radio-location equipment while making for Delamare Point on the south-east coast of Malta. They then turned north-east towards Sicily with the intention that the gliders would be released 4km short of the Maddalena promontory.

Every Horsa carried thirty-two men of the South Staffordshire Regiment together with their equipment, which included Bangalore torpedoes to be used for the destruction of barbed wire. The number of men in the Waco gliders varied from eighteen down to just four in those gliders that carried a jeep. Many of the gliders were released too early and over seventy fell in the sea, resulting in all those on board being drowned. Only eighty-seven troops reached their target area at Ponte Grande.

It is sobering to think that so many brave men who had survived the challenges of training at RAF Ringway in Manchester should have died without ever encountering the enemy. In the history books they are a mere footnote. Did the consequences of their incompetence ever trouble the consciences of the political leaders and military commanders?

The chaos of the Allied airborne invasion may have been confusing to the Allies, but it was even more baffling to the Axis commanders, who could not work out what the Allies were up to. They sent in reports saying that the invading force was between 20,000 to 30,000 strong when in fact it was just 4,600.

The beach landings were made in the early hours of 10 July at twenty-six points spread along 170km between the towns of Licata and Cassibile. The fierce winds made matters difficult, but also surprised the Axis forces, who had assumed that no one would attempt a landing in such poor conditions. By mid-morning, the Allies had captured Licata and the town of Syracuse.

On 11 July, Patton ordered a second airborne invasion involving 144 Dakotas and 2,000 troops east of Ponte Olivo. His aim was to block routes to the bridgehead at Gela. Throughout the day, German bombers had been buzzing the 7th Army landing area and the supporting fleet. They dropped strings of parachute flares, illuminating the ships with a brilliant blue-white glare, and circled overhead picking out their targets. The gun crews on the ships, half-blinded by the flares, fought back, filling the air with tracers, but the German planes were flying high, and the gunners could not see what they were shooting at.

Shortly after 10.30 p.m. it suddenly appeared to the gunners on the ships and to the crews of anti-aircraft batteries on shore that German aircraft were now coming in low, only a few hundred feet above the water, so low that their blue exhaust flames could be seen. More than 5,000 guns of all calibres opened up in an almighty blast of fire and smoke.

Cheering, the gunners watched several of the aircraft crash into the water or on to the beachhead. Out of other aircraft came parachutes and the gunners fired at the dark objects in the air. When one of the planes crashed close to the American destroyer USS *Beatty*, the gunners took no chances and pounded the wreckage with 20mm cannon fire until at last the plane was recognised for what it was: an American Dakota. In fact, all the low-flying planes were American. Twenty-three Dakotas were destroyed, and thirty-seven were badly damaged by this 'friendly fire'. One of the aircraft that somehow limped back to its base in North Africa had 1,000 holes in it. In all, 229 paratroopers were killed, wounded or left missing by their own side.

What had gone wrong? When Patton gave the order for the invasion, he instructed that all units should be notified and Major General Matthew B. Ridgway had flown to Sicily from North Africa to make sure that the warning order had been properly disseminated. Ridgway obtained assurances from the Navy commanders that the planes would not be fired on if they flew through a narrow corridor along the beachhead. The aircraft stuck to the prescribed corridor, but for reasons that have never been explained, some of the artillery units never received Ridgway's message. As Eisenhower pointed out in a post-mortem dispatch: 'The anti-aircraft gunners on ship and shore had been conditioned by two days of air attacks to shoot at sight.' (*Wallace, 1987*)

With or without adequate warning, the gunners very probably would have fired at the Dakotas, even though the planes were displaying the proper amber recognition lights. By arriving so soon after a German air raid, Patton's plan virtually guaranteed their destruction.

Later, after studying the disaster, General Ridgway concluded that the responsibility was: 'So divided, so difficult to fix. The losses are part of the inevitable price of war in human life.' (*Whiting, 1992*)

No one was to blame; no one was at fault. The innocent young lives lost pointlessly to incompetence, were just victims of the fortunes of war.

After landing, the US infantry took Ponte Olivo on 12 July and continued north, while the US troops on their right took the airfield at Comiso and entered Ragusa to link up with the Canadians. On the left, the troops who landed at Licata pushed 40km up the coast almost to Argento and 30km inland to Canicatti. Upon entering the town of Canicatti, American troops received a report that civilians were looting a bombed soap factory and filling up buckets with food and liquid soap. At around 6 p.m. Lieutenant Colonel George Herbert McCaffrey fired into the crowd after it failed to disperse. At least eight civilians, including an 11-year-old girl, were killed. This was just one of several war crimes committed by the Americans that was covered up at the time.

On 12 July, the German commander, Albert Kesselring,[31] concluded that the German formations needed to be reinforced, and that western Sicily should be abandoned so that he could strengthen the defence in the east. By contrast with the disciplined and battle-hardened German troops, the US troops were inexperienced and prone to indiscipline. Spooked by the killing of many of their comrades at the hands of German and Italian machine guns, they had a thirst for revenge.

On 14 July, American troops captured forty-five Brescian and Venetian soldiers from northern Italy and three German PoWs while attacking an airfield near Santo Pietro. Major Roger Denman ordered Sergeant Horace T. West to take that group of prisoners: 'To the rear, off the road, where they would not be conspicuous, and hold them for questioning.' (*Kuroski, 2016*)

Stripped of their shirts and shoes, West marched the soldiers for about a mile before directing that eight or nine be separated from the rest and taken to the regiment's intelligence officer for questioning. Left to guard the remaining thirty-seven, West turned to his men and said: 'Now I'm killing these motherfuckers.' He then seized a Tommy gun and turned it on the PoWs, telling the other American soldiers to 'turn around if you don't want to see it'. Three prisoners managed to escape (who lived to tell the tale). The others were cut down as they called for mercy. West himself finished off those who were still breathing.

The next day, the thirty-seven bodies were seen by an American military chaplain, Lieutenant Colonel William E. King, who reported the incident to his superiors. At first it was dismissed through fear of the bad press that might result if it were made public. However, after some convincing, senior officers agreed to court martial West. He was eventually sentenced to life imprisonment but was released back to active service in November 1944 as a private, and honourably discharged at the end of the war. No one was guilty; no one was to blame.

On the same day, Captain John T. Compton, who had landed south of the Acate river, was simply 'too excited to sleep for three days after the invasion'. (*Harris, 2009*) On the fourth day, he managed about an hour and a half of sleep before taking part in an attack on the Biscari airfield. On reaching the airfield, Compton and his men began to receive

31 Albert Kesselring (30 November 1885–16 July 1960) commanded Luftwaffe forces in the German invasions of Poland and France, the Battle of Britain and the invasion of the Soviet Union. As Wehrmacht Commander-in-Chief South, he was the overall German commander in the Mediterranean theatre, which included the North African campaign.

artillery, mortar, and sniper fire that targeted wounded American soldiers as well as the medics attempting to aid them. Out of the thirty-four men in Compton's Platoon, twelve were either wounded or killed.

When thirty-five Italians, some in civilian clothing, were found sheltering in a cave, Compton said bluntly, 'Get them shot.' He told the American soldiers to line up and they positioned themselves about 2m away from the prisoners. Seeing that their fate was sealed, a few of them tried to run, but the firing squad opened fire and killed them all. Compton was charged subsequently with killing forty prisoners in his charge but was acquitted and transferred to another regiment.[32] No one was to blame; it was just the fortunes of war.

Meanwhile, the British 8th Army was bogged down. *Operation Fustian* was an attempt by Montgomery to capture the Primosole Bridge over the River Simeto. The intention was for glider-borne paratroopers to land on both sides of the river and then capture the bridge and secure the surrounding area until they could be relieved by the British troops who had landed three days before. Because the bridge was the only crossing on the river, this would give the British 8th Army access to the Catania plain.

However, many of the American aircraft that towed the gliders from North Africa were shot down or hit by friendly fire from American gunners, causing them to turn back. When the planes bearing the cargoes of dead and dying paratroopers arrived back at their bases in North Africa, there was great anger among the British, and the remaining troops and surviving glider pilots of the British 1st Airborne Division had to be confined to camp in order to prevent a mass 'slugfest' with the US pilots. (*Whiting, 1992*)

Those gliders that managed to land in Sicily scattered the troops over a large area but they succeeded in capturing the bridge. They also managed to repulse Axis counterattacks and held out until nightfall. The relief force was just 1.6km away when they halted for the night. By this time, with casualties mounting and supplies running short, the paratroopers had to relinquish control of the bridge to the Germans. The following day the British troops, with tank support, attempted to recapture it, but they did not achieve their goal until three days later. Even then the capture of Primosole Bridge did not lead to the expected rapid advance, because by this time the Germans had gathered their forces and established a new defensive line.

On 16 July, the surviving Italian Air Force aircraft withdrew to the mainland as Montgomery renewed his attack toward Catania. The British

32 Ironically, he died in November 1943 while fighting in the Italian campaign.

troops met strong opposition and by 19 July Montgomery decided to call off the attack. The Canadians continued to advance, but it was becoming clear that, as German units settled into their new positions in north-eastern Sicily, the Allies did not have sufficient strength to overcome them. The Canadians were ordered to divert north to Leonforte and then turn eastward to Adrano on the south-western slopes of Mount Etna.

By 17 July, American troops under Patton had captured Porto Empedocle and Agrigento. Alexander then issued further orders to Patton to push eastward along the coast road to capture Palermo, the regional capital of Sicily. Patton's troops, under Major General Lucien K. Truscott, achieved this objective on 22 July having covered 100 miles in seventy-two hours without facing any serious opposition.

Palermo was the first city liberated by US forces in the Second World War and, according to British author Raleigh Trevelyan, the American soldiers were surprised by their warm reception. Women kissed and hugged the men while jeeps, trucks, and tanks were showered with flowers, almonds, apples and lemons. In some places policemen had to hold back the enthusiastic crowd. When the surrender was made official, Patton entered the city at the head of an armoured column as Sicilian civilians cheered 'Down with Mussolini!' and 'Long live America!' (*Trevelyan, 1981*)

With the fighting in Sicily still raging, more than 500 Allied bombers struck Rome for the first time, hitting the San Lorenzo freight yard and steel factory, as well as the Littorio and Ciampino airports. Bombs also hit the Basilica of San Lorenzo, and graves in the Campo Verano cemetery. As many as 3,000 people were killed. The people of Rome had grown weary of the war and of two decades of fascist rule, but these air raids were a final straw. The economy was in crisis, industry was crippled, and rations had been cut to 900 calories a day so that more food could be sent to Germany. The decisive event, even more compelling, were the stories that were circulating about the success of the Allied campaign in Sicily. By mid-July it was clear that nothing could stop the Allies from overrunning the island.

This success gave Eisenhower confidence that perhaps Churchill's idea of an invasion of mainland Italy might not have been such a bad idea after all. Eisenhower's naval aide, Harry C. Butcher, wrote that on 18 July:

> Ike … drafted a recommendation to the Combined Chiefs of Staff that as soon as we take Messina we proceed across the Strait to the toe of Italy. The gist of this recommendation is that we carry the war to the mainland and the attack on the toe and ball would be accomplished by other landings and perhaps an attack on Naples. (*Butcher, 1946*)

Chapter 14

ARREST OF MUSSOLINI AND THE ITALIAN ARMISTICE

On 24 July 1943, Mussolini was summoned by the Fascist Grand Council and the following day he was removed from government by King Victor Emmanuel III and placed under arrest. When Mussolini was told by Field Marshal Pietro Badoglio that the Fascist Grand Council intended to seek an armistice, Mussolini turned to the King and said: 'Then my ruin is complete.' (*Wallace, 1987*) When Hitler received the news, he was furious and he recalled Rommel from Greece and gave him overall responsibility for German forces in Italy.

The Italian armistice with the Allies was duly signed in Cassibile on behalf of Badoglio, who was made Prime Minister of Italy. Having been dismissed by the King, Mussolini went out to the Villa Savoia in Rome, ending the twenty-one years of his dictatorship.

Hitler's first impulse was to order his troops to seize Rome, the King and the Royal Family, but Rommel dissuaded him from this. Hitler then instructed Rommel to find out where Mussolini was being held and to rescue him. He also ordered his generals to stand by to execute '*Plan Achse*' (Axis Project), a scheme whereby German soldiers were to disarm the Italian military and take over the coastal defences.

Mussolini's sudden removal from power surprised the Allies, and Eisenhower decided that he could now withdraw seven divisions – four American and three British – from the Mediterranean and send them to England to prepare for the cross-Channel landings that were being planned for the following spring.

Eisenhower thought that the best he could do in Italy was to try to seize the German-occupied islands of Sardinia and Corsica. Their capture would not represent a great triumph, but at least it could be accomplished with the resources available, and the islands could serve as bases for further bombing attacks on central and northern Italy. Another possibility might be to invade the toe and heel of the Italian boot and then push north cautiously. His first thoughts were that an ambitious campaign against the Italian mainland was not possible.

However, Eisenhower's advisers managed to convince him that an amphibious assault on the Italian mainland near Naples might be viable. Churchill was delighted with this shift of strategy. However, the capture of Rome – one of the world's great cities, and the seat of the Fascist government – would be a great victory both politically and psychologically. Churchill had not been impressed with the plan to take Corsica and Sardinia, nor did he care for the more cautious push from the toe of Italy. As he wrote later: 'Why crawl up the leg like a harvest bug from the ankle upwards? Let us rather strike at the knee.' (*Webb, 1969*)

Churchill was pleased to find himself supported in this view by George Marshall, who had previously insisted that the Mediterranean was a sideshow. Marshall had not really changed his mind at all, but he had come to believe that if Churchill did not get his way, he might insist on keeping major British forces in the Mediterranean until he did, thereby further impeding a cross-Channel invasion.

While the Allies hurried ahead with plans to exploit Mussolini's fall from power, Badoglio sent messengers to contact British diplomats in Lisbon to begin what Eisenhower described as 'a series of negotiations, secret communications, clandestine journeys by secret agents, and frequent meetings in hidden places that, if encountered in the fictional world, would have been scorned as incredible melodrama'. (*Eisenhower, 2012*)

Churchill was sceptical and he observed: 'Badoglio admits that he is going to double-cross someone and I have no intention of being the victim.' (*Annussek, 2005*) However, Badoglio's furtiveness can be explained by his deep fear of German retaliation for Italy's defection. It was possible, indeed likely, that he and the entire Italian royal family might be arrested and executed.

Rome remained in German hands for the next nine months, and during this period the suppression of the Roman people was often brutal. Jews, anti-Fascists and royalists became targets for persecution. The Vatican became a controlled enclave, with Nazi sentries posted at the entrance to St Peter's Square, as the German troops requisitioned food and fuel. There was an undercurrent of fear of being arrested on the street.

Back on Sicily, Montgomery was now gathering his forces to renew the attack on Adrano, while by 7 August, the US troops had captured

Mount Pellegrino, which overlooked the Axis defences at Troina. These advances allowed the Allied artillery to target the Axis forces with great accuracy. The tide was beginning to turn. Kesselring reported to Hitler on 29 July that an evacuation across the Messina Straits could be accomplished in three days and he began to plan for this eventuality.

Kesselring then mounted a range of delaying tactics. His plan was thorough and well-thought out, with clear lines of command imposing strict discipline on the operation. The full-scale withdrawal, code-named *Operation Lehrgang,* began on 11 August and continued to 17 August. During this period, the Germans kept the Allies at arm's length with the use of mines, demolitions and other obstacles.

As a result, the Allies were not able to prevent or delay the German ships that carried the forces and equipment across the Strait of Messina. The narrow straits were protected by 120 heavy and 112 light anti-aircraft guns and the resulting overlapping gunfire from both sides of the strait made daylight air attacks highly hazardous and generally unsuccessful.

There were times when night-time air attacks were able to delay traffic across the Straits, but when daylight returned the Germans were able to clear the backlog from the previous night. The hazards of a strong current and fear that Italian warships might make suicide runs prevented the Allies from risking their warships in the Straits. By 18 August, the Germans had evacuated 52,000 troops (including 4,444 wounded), 14,105 vehicles, 47 tanks, 94 guns, 1,100 tons of ammunition and about 20,700 tons of gear and stores.

***

But I am getting ahead of myself again. The invasion of Sicily was like a radio playing in a distant room. I could hear the noise and even caught the odd word, but I had no understanding of what was happening beyond the partial and overly optimistic accounts in the (heavily censored) newspapers, of which this account was typical:

> Catania is about to fall, and Axis troops are reported to be evacuating the town. There is pessimism in Berlin. There is a general Axis retreat northward. The enemy's resistance does not appear to be organised at all except along the eastern coast, where the front is held by German troops on the two wings, with the Italians in the centre. Aerial reconnaissance has confirmed that the Axis forces have started a general retreat towards Messina and that they are streaming northwards along every road and railway still in use. (*Liverpool Echo*, 1943)

We thought the Germans were on the run. How wrong we all were!

Chapter 15

MUNDESLEY AND THE ROYAL BERKSHIRES

On arrival back at Colchester, I had two weeks without doing too much but wait for my posting. It came through eventually. I was posted to the 9th Battalion of the Royal Berkshire Regiment, a holding battalion based in Norfolk.

We took the train from Colchester to Norwich, where we changed on to a branch line for North Walsham, and then Mundesley. Here we were taken by Army transport to our destination and received a shock to find we were going to be billeted in bell tents surrounded by trees and magnificent rhododendron shrubs in the grounds of a stately home that served as the Company HQ.

We were soon set to undergo further rigorous training involving long 'carries' with the mortar gun. The distance of the carry was in the region of 5km, and this had to be completed in a set time. The only way to achieve this time was to run with the mortar. Bearing in mind that each piece of the mortar weighed in the region of 18kg and the fact that we had to cope with the heat of high summer, this was energy sapping.

After a couple of weeks, we were moved on from the bell tents to an old holiday camp at Mundesley, just a few miles away. We were told that this would be our last stopping point until we were posted abroad. We were promised that we would be allowed a further period of leave before we embarked, and this was duly granted.

On our return from leave, they issued us with warm weather kit, and we started to think that we might be destined for the Far East. Then there was an about turn. It was decided that those of us who were under 21 were too young to be sent abroad. As a result, underage soldiers like me were formed into a new platoon and told that we would be required to undergo another six more weeks of infantry training with the Wiltshire Regiment before being eligible for overseas service.

The training regime with the Wiltshires was hard but not unduly arduous. We did a 10,000m (6-mile) run and walk in full battle order, then a 16,000m (10-mile) run and walk. These had to be completed in one and two hours respectively. We also climbed up and down the sand cliffs on Mundesley beach, which were over 30m high and dangerous in places.

As our six weeks' training were ending, one or two of the men in the platoon broached the subject of leave before our embarkation. The officer promised to ask the company commander. We waited in expectation for the officer to report back, and when he did, we were somewhat shocked that there would be no leave for us. To say the least, we were very dejected at the news. On seeing our faces, the lieutenant asked us:

> Have I your permission to approach the company commander and tell him, without any thought of mutiny in the ranks, that the men will go abroad with very bad feeling after the promise made to them in good faith was broken? (*Vere, 2006*)

He duly did as he had promised and returned to us immediately to tell us that the company commander had sanctioned our embarkation leave without question.

On our return from leave, we had a kit inspection and once again we were kitted out with clothes, which suggested that we were heading for somewhere hot. We were then confined to the camp having been told that we would be leaving very soon.

We moved out of the camp in transports on 2 August 1943, Bank Holiday Monday. We were taken to the station and boarded the train without having any idea where we were heading. The train passed from daylight into darkness and back again. Then someone recognised that we had just passed Carlisle. We soon arrived at the Scottish border and the penny dropped; we were on our way to the port of Glasgow.

The train rumbled on until we arrived in Glasgow with its workshops and warehouses. Finally, we came to a halt at the end of the line. We moved off the train with all our gear, formed up in threes and marched off along the quay that contained a ship with a noticeable tilt in dry dock. It was a strange sight. We were halted alongside the ship and ordered to file aboard. We weren't travelling on this ship. It had been torpedoed in the Atlantic Ocean and had limped home to go into dry dock and was now awaiting repairs to her damaged hull. This was going to be our billet, under the stars on the mess decks.

Two days later, our transport ship arrived in dock, and it was not long before we were transferred on board. The name of the ship was the SS *Bergensfjord*,[33] an ocean liner that had sailed for the Norwegian America Line before the war and which had been requisitioned by the Ministry of War Transport for use as a troop ship. It was not long before other men joined us; it was going to be a very tight squeeze for us all.

Before we set off, the officer in charge came over the loudspeakers to say that he understood we were short on space. He told us that we would have to make the best of it for the sake of the war effort. We would soon be joining the convoy, and he expected each of us to play his part.

---

33 SS *Bergensfjord* had embarked on her last journey from Bergen to New York on 7 April 1940, only two days before the German invasion of Norway. On arrival in New York she was laid up, but she was requisitioned by the British Ministry of War Transport in November 1940 and converted to a troop ship over the following months.

Chapter 16

AUGUST 1943 LEAVING FOR ITALY

On my 21st birthday, 14 August 1943, I was sailing down the Clyde without any certainty about where I was heading, but I was already convinced in my mind that our destination was Italy.

As the ship sailed on, a few of the men began singing popular songs such as 'There'll Always Be an England' and 'We'll Meet Again'. I was morose and not in the mood for singing. As I looked at the shoreline, I wondered about my chances of surviving should I jump overboard and swim to the shore. As the speed of the ship increased and the distance increased, I decided better of it.

As the last bit of the coastline disappeared, the men sang 'It's a Lovely Day Tomorrow'. This last song was thoroughly sentimental, but to me a wholly inappropriate choice. How could we possibly feel positive about the future when all we could think about was the horrors ahead of us? There were few men who were not affected. After the song had ended, somebody said quietly 'that's that' and silence then prevailed.

In the morning, things soon settled down into an organised routine. Meal sittings were staggered and there were daily parades for each unit for physical training and lectures. The ship's broadcasting system was used constantly, not only for conveying orders and messages, but also for playing gramophone records, of which they had a large stock. The voyage was peaceful and untroubled and there was plenty of opportunity to enjoy the fresh air and sunshine on deck, to watch the manoeuvres of the convoy and escorting destroyers, and to read.

During that week we still had little idea about our destination, but the rumours grew that it must be somewhere in Italy. One afternoon we were ordered to muster on the upper deck to hear a speech by the ship's captain, thanking everyone for the efforts so far made to ensure the success of the operation. He told us that we had another week on the ship and concluded with the words 'the best of luck to you all in Italy'.

At last, we knew, and this announcement was soon followed by the official news on 25 August 1943 that I had been assigned to the 56th London Division of the 10th Battalion of the Royal Berkshire Regiment, with its emblem of a black cat on a red background. We were to be part of the US 5th Army, and we were to make an assault landing at Salerno in the early hours of the following Sunday morning as part of a great operation.

During this last week on the ship there were many briefings and preparations for the landings. Talks were given, both by our own unit officers and by intelligence officers, giving us some idea as to what we should expect on landing and thereafter. We were warned not to be too optimistic about a peaceful reception. German reaction to the invasion was expected to be swift and immediate. As each day passed, we were supplied with more details about our part in the coming operation, and we were all required to make a rough sketch map of our 'beach' and the surrounding area (in case we got lost, I suppose!).

At mid-afternoon on the Friday, I saw the first bit of land for ten days. This was the south-western coast of Spain. The convoy passed through the Straits of Gibraltar at about midnight. Coming up on deck on Saturday morning, I watched the ships moving through the calm blue waters of the Mediterranean in an easterly, and later in a westerly direction. Constant manoeuvres of this sort were all part of the tactics of the convoy.

I was resting in the sunshine on the deck with several others, when I was startled by a sudden voice through the loudspeakers: 'Attention please! Enemy aircraft approaching Starboard bow!'

In a few seconds a terrific barrage was put up by the guns of the ships in our convoy. The enemy planes were not around for long, but we had obviously been spotted and that made us all very jumpy.

As darkness fell on the Saturday evening, the convoy was moving off the coast of Algeria. We were told that 'zero hour' would be at midnight for the first of the troops who would be making an assault on Algiers. Others would follow once a beachhead had been established. We approached Algiers at 11 p.m. and orders were given to the men in the lower decks over the ship's broadcasting system: 'Synchronise all watches. Keep all gangways clear.'

I managed to grab a few moments' sleep, fully dressed, in my hammock only to be woken up just after midnight by the noise of the disembarkation of the first group of American Rangers. I went to see them off with their faces blackened. 'Good luck, boys all the best!' we wished them as they went up on deck. A few minutes later I watched them boarding the small landing craft positioned around the sides of the ship. They all looked petrified and nothing like the smart-talking, wise-cracking GIs of those Hollywood war films.

The ship had now anchored, and there was no sound from its engines and no moonlight. In the distance and through the darkness I could see the lights of Algiers. The last of the men had boarded the landing craft and they were off. Then, complete silence.

Ormond Yard, Holborn, where my father lived.

Men of the Army Veterinary Corps (AVC).

The Bells, Drury Lane where I was born © London Archives.

Covent Garden Market porters 1930.

With my sister Nora, brother Bert and two friends hop-picking at Sandhurst.

Back to Sandhurst with Nora, 60 years later.

ANOTHER DEATH FROM WALL COLLAPSE

Two Other Bristol Men Injured

One man was killed and two were injured when a wall collapsed in Old Temple Street, Bristol, yesterday while a demolition party was at work.

From papers in his possession the dead man is believed to be G. H. Meadows, of Broad Walk, Knowle.

The injured, whose condition is stated not to be serious, are James Feely (30), of Christiana Terrace, Hotwells, injuries to right thigh, and Thomas Bricker (39), of Greenbank Avenue, Easton, injuries to ribs, legs and hands.

Mr Feely, and acetylene welder, was at work when the collapse occurred. "I jumped for it," he said, but some of the falling masonry caught him as he leapt.

The St. John Ambulance took the injured men to the Bristol Royal Infirmary.

Western Daily Press May 1942.

Living it up in Bristol.

Hero of the Blitz.

Bren gun carrier driver training.

My crew at Mundesley on board our Bren gun carrier.

British 3 inch mortar.

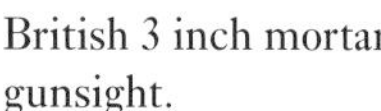

British 3 inch mortar gunsight.

British 3 inch mortar shell.

Army Form A. 2038.

Identification Card for Mechanical Transport Drivers.

THE WAR OFFICE.

The undersigned..

(description)..

....

being employed on Military Service, is hereby authorized by the Secretary of State for War to drive a motor car, lorry, motor cycle or other mechanically propelled vehicle when on Government duty.

....
Signature of Holder.

Permanent Under-Secretary of State for War.

Available from..to..

(16531) Wt.33875/1199 500,000 12/40 A.& E.W.Ltd. Gp.698 Forms/A.2038/5.

My first Driving Licence.

A 15-cwt Fordson truck in which I learned to drive.

SS *Bergensfjord* that took me to Italy.

HS *Llandovery Castle* that brought me home.

Entering Salerno, September 1943. © Imperial War Museums.

My comrades on the slopes of Monte Camino. © Imperial War Museums.

A whaler of the same type as HMS *Santa*.

My brother Jimmy on board HMS *Santa* at Alexandria.

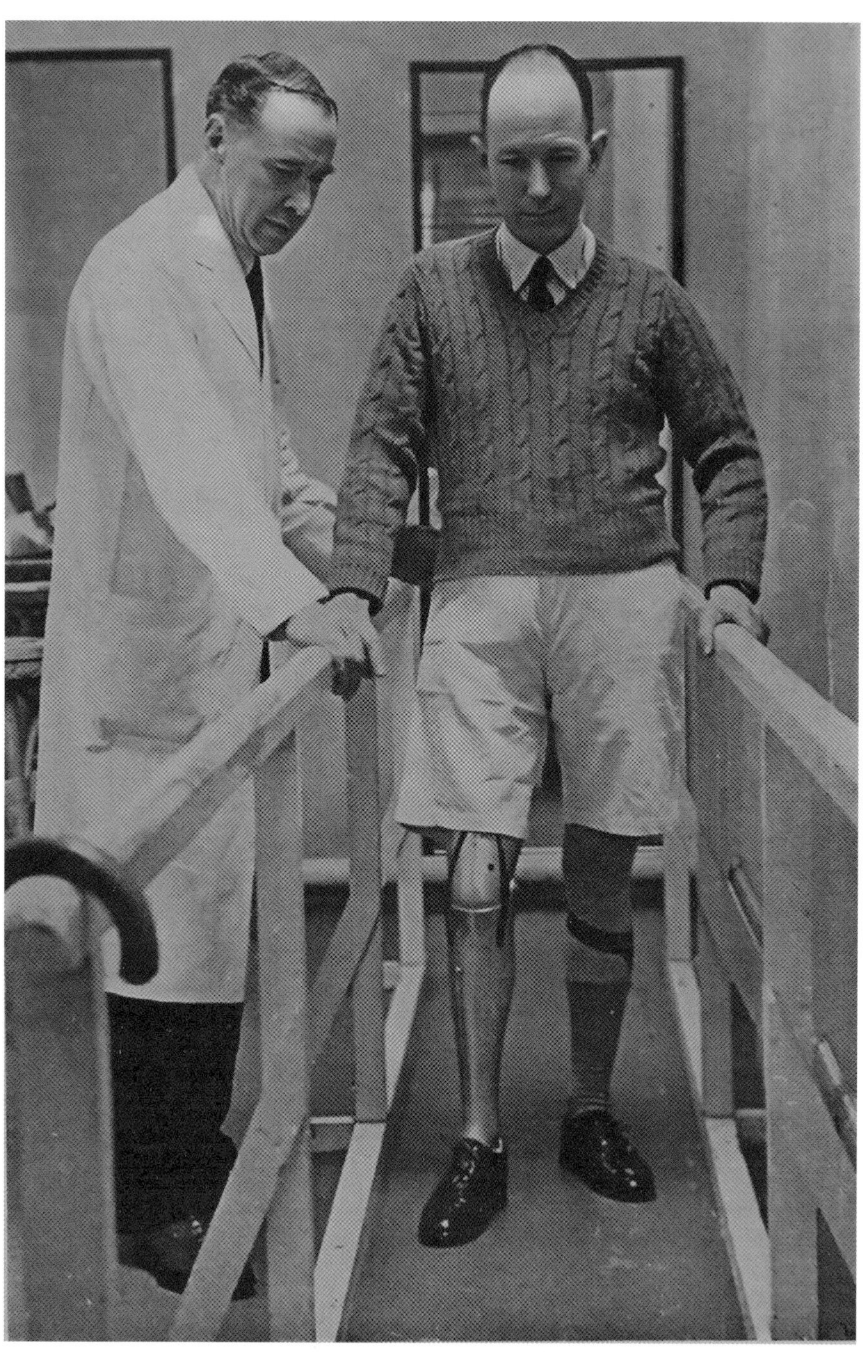

One of my fellow amputees learning to walk at Roehampton.

Our Wedding.

My beautiful wife, Maisie.

With my nephew, Danny.

At the Ministry of Pensions, Redhill.

My mother and father in 1960.

My three children: Michael, John and Sharon.

Chapter 17

WOUNDED

When the Allied commanders discussed the plans for the invasion, they recognised that it was likely that there would be heavy Allied casualties. The extent of the casualties would be determined by the speed with which the beachhead could be secured. The planners hoped that if the beachhead could be established quickly it would then be possible for the Allied forces to march on Rome. Memories of the Great War and the attrition in Flanders were still comparatively fresh and the planners urged that, at all costs, Allied forces were to avoid getting bogged down in a stalemate.

However, even the assumptions underpinning the strategy were contradictory. The chief purpose of the invasion was to divert German men and material from the Eastern Front to help Stalin and from northern France to assist with the planned invasion, but that would mean fighting a war on four fronts: on the Eastern front, across the Channel, in the Pacific and in Italy, something that the Allies had previously agreed was unwise. They had banked everything on the Germans stopping north of Rome. When Hitler pushed troops south through the Brenner Pass, the Allied strategy fell apart.

Even when this flaw became obvious, Churchill was in no mood for second thoughts or regrets, as his personal physician, Lord Moran, wrote in his diary:

> When the attack on Sicily was well under way I wanted to know whether Germany meant to put up a stiff resistance in southern Italy or whether she would decide to retire to the Po as Winston suggested. I wanted more facts. I wanted to ask Winston a dozen questions, but he gave me no chance. He kept telling me what was going to happen. All wishing and guessing. When I did get a question in, the Prime Minister brushed it aside. I tried to set forth some of the factors which ought

> to govern our decision. I tried to argue that we must exercise great discretion in choosing what to do after the conquest of Sicily. I said to the Prime Minister that I would be content if Sardinia were taken before the invasion of France. He replied that the difference between taking southern Italy and Sardinia was the difference between a glorious campaign and a mere convenience. (*Wilson, 1966*)

The Allied invasion plan that emerged called for Montgomery and the British 8th Army to cross the Strait of Messina between 30 August and 4 September. The timing was left to Montgomery, although Eisenhower hoped the crossing would be made as soon as practical. This was because on 9 September the US 5th Army – of which I was now part – would make the main assault at Salerno. It was planned that additional British troops in the 8th Army would land at Taranto on the heel of Italy, to secure that port and drive north toward Naples. Although the 8th Army and the 5th Army would be 200 miles apart and, therefore, too far away to enable them to support each other immediately, it was hoped that the 8th Army could advance rapidly to help if the Salerno landing ran into trouble.

The British 8th Army, under Montgomery, landed in the toe of Italy across the Messina Straits on 3 September 1943 in *Operation Baytown*. On the same day the Italian government directed all Italian troops to end hostilities. When the armistice was announced on 8 September 1943, cries of 'Viva la pace!' (Long live peace!) rang through the streets.

By mid-afternoon on 8 September 1943 the Germans became aware that a fleet of some 500 Allied ships was heading in their direction. The main Allied effort was led by Mark Clark[34] and the US 5th Army, initially centred on the port of Naples. Mark Clark was a tall New Yorker with supreme self-confidence. Churchill called him 'the American Eagle' and wrote later that 'nobody could control Mark Clark, he controlled himself'. (*Trevelyan, 1981*)

Naples was selected as a target because it was the northernmost port that could receive air cover by fighter planes flying from Sicily. It was also hoped that anti-fascist fighters might be able to sustain a disruptive guerilla campaign until Allied forces arrived.

For a while, Montgomery's 8th Army was able to make relatively easy progress up the east coast, capturing the port of Bari and the important airfields around Foggia. There was a hope that, with the

34 Mark Wayne Clark (1 May 1896–17 April 1984) had served as a company commander in France in the Great War and suffered serious wounds from shrapnel.

surrender of the Italian government, the Germans would withdraw to the north. Complacency and a lack of due respect began to set in. Montgomery told his troops: 'These Italians are a rotten crowd. They just lie among their grapes and lemons and breed. Far too many of them. That's the trouble. Far too many of them.' (*Trevelyan, 1981*)

Montgomery and Churchill had visions of sweeping onwards to Rome largely unchallenged and if innocent Italian farmers and their families were killed in the process, it was their lookout.

However, the optimism was premature. Hitler was furious about this act of betrayal and, fearing for their lives, Badoglio, King Victor Emmanuel, some military ministers, and the Chief of the General Staff escaped to Pescara and Brindisi in the early hours of 9 September 1943. Italian Army, Navy, and Air Force commanders were surprised to be confronted by German officers demanding that they hand over their weapons and supplies under *Operation Achse*. This was perceived by the population of Rome[35] as undignified; an act of cowardice that compounded the so-called 'Morte della Patria' (the death of the fatherland) and the loss of national pride associated with Italy's surrender. Within hours, the Germans entered Rome and announced the imposition of German military law with summary execution for violators.

While all this was taking place, the SS *Bergensfjord* was landing at the port of Bizerte in Tunisia. We docked there on 9 September 1943 as this was to be our staging post prior to our landing at Salerno. We stayed at the camp for a few days, and then were told to get ready for the invasion. We were not in the first wave and so we had a lot of waiting around. The delay was exacerbated by the fact that the ships had to be loaded in such a way that vehicles and equipment would arrive in Salerno Bay in the order that they were needed to secure the beachhead. A mistake in the loading of one ship would have made many changes necessary on other ships.

After several idle hours we left the camp in lorries for our short journey down to the docks, stopping at a row of American LCI landing craft ships that were going to take us across over 300 miles of open sea that was teeming with Italian and German ships and submarines. It was a chilling thought.

Once on board the flat-bottomed ships, we were each given a tin of bully beef for the journey and a lifejacket. Our ship felt the full

---

35 The north of Italy remained firmly under German control, and Mussolini was still head of the Italian Social Republic until April 1945.

force of the swell of the Mediterranean and several of the men were seasick, but the trip was otherwise uneventful. We learned later that the Italian Navy had already surrendered, and the Royal Navy was able to provide cover in strength sufficient to deter the Germans.

After the long choppy sea voyage, we arrived at Vietri just north of Salerno. Our ship ran up on to the sandy beach and we stepped ashore untroubled, barely getting our feet wet. Fortunately for us, the Royal Marines who had landed before us had cleared out all of the German defenders.

We were then marched off in the direction of the town. We were conscious that our landing was a lot easier than those that happened just a few short weeks ago at Sicily and we all felt grateful. As evening fell on 9 September 1943, more than 50,000 of us came ashore and had pushed inland as the Germans retreated to the port of Naples, over 30 miles away.

It was then that we heard the announcement of the surrender of Italy. This news was greeted with mass cheering and jubilation. For a few fleeting moments we thought that the collapse of the Axis was imminent and that the end of the war was in sight before we had encountered the enemy. How foolish we were!

On the Salerno beachhead I was assigned to a three-man mortar crew. We were then allocated a Bren gun carrier and ordered to drive to Salerno town. Along the roadside, we saw recently dug graves marked by plain wooden crosses indicating that British soldiers were buried there. We learned later that the Royal Marines, who had gone on ahead of us, had encountered heavy machine gun fire from the flooded dykes, fields and tall tobacco plants along the roads that had provided excellent cover for German snipers. They had suffered heavily to make the route safer for us.

In the town, we were directed to our billet. We could hardly miss it. We were assigned to the magnificent Guiseppi Verdi Municipal Theatre at Piazza Matteo Luciani: the Salerno Opera house. It was a grand nineteenth-century building with an ornate façade. We were told to bed down on the backstage area, which was vast, but with a good deal of machinery for pulling the backdrops and lifting the safety curtain. It was not entirely dissimilar to the backstage at the Prince's Theatre but the incongruity of being there in combat uniform and ready to go into battle gave me no comfort at all. Where I lay, I could see the props from a recent production of Verdi's *Aida.* I can't claim to be an opera buff, but I was very familiar with the most famous operas that were performed just round the corner from where I had worked in the Market. I thought to myself: 'Well, at least I can tell my mother that I had been on the stage of an Italian opera house.'

I still had part of my bully beef ration left and realised that this would have to keep me going until the next day. I then settled down to a night of broken, dream-filled sleep. Next day, we were given a decent meal, which several of us ate outside in the sun. A small boy who was just skin and bone approached us repeating: 'Per favore, posso avere del cibo? Ho fame.' None of us could speak Italian, but we were left in no doubt about what he was saying as he pointed back and forth from his mouth to his stomach. I offered him some of my bully beef and I have never seen anyone so happy. Every day after that, he appeared whenever I came out of the opera house, and I took to saving him something from every meal.

Just 10 miles further up the coast the situation was quite different for the US troops who landed in *Operation Avalanche*. The shore was divided into four sectors, from north to south, identified as 'Red', 'Green', 'Yellow' and 'Blue' beaches. At least two nights before, Navy frogmen had marked out the four sectors on the shore with coloured lights that matched the colour of the designated beach. These lights were designed to guide the landing craft to their appropriate beach, but they were also helpful to the German defenders in that they showed where they should direct their guns.

The US troops were met with heavy machine gun fire as they tried to land. There was no element of surprise and no pre-invasion naval bombardment. This was because the US Commander, General Fred Walker, had not asked for one. He feared that the naval guns might hit his own men. In his memoirs he also confessed to an unusually rare, but humane motive: 'There are a few old emplacements back from the beach, but there are no appropriate targets for navy gunfire, and I see no point to killing a lot of peaceful Italians and destroying their homes.' (*Walker, 1969*)

Laudable though his decision was, it deprived his men of the psychological boost that a heavy naval bombardment would have given. It also represented a misjudgement. The 'few old emplacements' were all manned by German machine gunners.

It was noon before the main tank assault began and it soon ground to a standstill on the beaches and most of the fighting had to be done by the infantry. The men had to crawl through barbed wire while machine gun fire whistled over their heads. Some of them tried to dig foxholes in the shallows in the face of intense fire but more than 200 men never made it off those beaches.

To make matters worse, the Germans did not withdraw. Instead, Kesselring ordered reinforcements to strengthen the German defences. To counter the build-up of German troops, Mark Clark ordered his floating reserve to provide support in the hope that the British 8th Army would be able to press on and provide relief from the south. However, the rugged terrain and German sabotage posed serious problems, as Montgomery wrote later:

> The roads in Southern Italy twist and turn in the mountainous country and are admirable feats of engineering. They abound in bridges, viaducts, culverts and even tunnels and this offers unlimited scope to military engineers for demolitions and roadblocks of every conceivable kind. The Germans took the fullest advantage of this fact and our advance throughout was barred and delayed by demolitions on the widest possible scale. (*Wallace, 1987*)

On 13 September – 'Black Monday' as it became known – the US troops tried desperately to claw their way out of the beachhead, but the Germans still commanded the high ground. In addition, German tanks were now massing in the hills and striking at weak points all along the Allied lines. Clark realised that he was now facing an ignominious defeat, and he made arrangements so that the US troops could be evacuated at ten minutes' notice if necessary.

In his increasing anxiety, Clark expressed frustration with the slow progress being made by the British 8th Army. When he received a message from Montgomery saying: 'Hold on, we've joined hands,' he replied: 'If we've joined hands, I haven't felt a thing yet.' (*Adelman, 1968*)

All through 14 September the Germans attacked, knowing that victory was now within their grasp, but by now additional Allied artillery and infantry had landed on the beaches and had started to dig in. Allied artillery gun crews were now firing as many as ten rounds per minute from hundreds of heavy howitzers and Mark Clark moved along the line of gunners to give them encouragement. Under this onslaught, the tide slowly began to turn and Kesselring ordered his divisions to pull back to higher ground to fight another day. By sunset their retreat was complete and by 15 September the beachhead had been secured – six days after the initial landings. It had been a remarkably close call. Two days later the 5th and the 8th Armies finally linked up. Montgomery had the good grace to admit to his chief of staff:

> Some would like to think – I did at the time – that we helped, if not saved the situation at Salerno, but now I doubt whether we influenced matters to any great extent. General Clark had everything under control before the 8th Army appeared. (*Guingand, 1947*)

While all this was going on we were marking time in the relative peace and quiet of Salerno town. However, it wasn't long before we received orders that we were to move to the next staging camp, at Castellammare, just a few miles away. When we got there, we found that our billet was in a large railway wagon yard and that we were to sleep in some of the railway wagons. Our wagon was no comparison to the opera house, but it could have been worse. Although the yard was dirty and industrial, it had a rather grand hall that was once a dining room for the men who worked in the yard. I'll never forget its beautiful, tiled floor. One of the jobs that we were given to keep us busy was to wash this floor thoroughly with seawater collected from the nearby sandy beach. After washing it with sea water, we went over it again with clear, fresh water drawn from a large well. I rather enjoyed seeing the tiles restored to pristine condition.

On several evenings while we were at the yard, we were entertained with Neapolitan folksong by some Italian singers and musicians. I absolutely loved their music, and we always gave them tremendous applause. We also sent round a hat, which usually raised several thousand Italian lire by the end of the evening. It was the least we could do because the war meant that all these men were unemployed and without another any other income.

The large workshop in the yard where the wagons had been repaired had been vandalised. It wasn't obvious to us who was responsible for this. Salerno was then in a state of chaos and close to collapse. The people were hungry, angry and confused. I can't say that they were particularly pleased to see us. I think they saw us as just another oppressor.

In the morning, I was ordered to take the Bren gun carrier and follow the convoy. I had no idea where we were heading. We were passing through Saraceri when it started to rain, cold slanting rain. Before we had gone a mile or so in this downpour, the Bren gun carrier developed an engine problem, and we had to stop. By the time we had got it started again there was no sign of the convoy. We got back on board, and I pressed on as fast as the carrier would carry us until we came to a fork in the road. It wasn't clear which road to take, so I took the left-hand turn. We were soon halted by a British soldier: 'Turn round, you fool, the Jerries are only two hundred yards down there!' I stopped immediately and executed the fastest about turn I have ever managed!

We retraced our route, took the right-hand fork and eventually caught the rest of the convoy of lorries and carriers that had come to a halt. This was obviously our destination, but it looked like the middle of nowhere! We climbed out of the Bren gun carrier into the rain-swept night and followed the trail of men up a track through a wood of chestnut trees. The track was steep in places, and we were now emotionally and physically tired with the stress, the wet, the cold and the physical exertion of lugging the mortar gun and bombs to the crest of the hill. I suppose the peak of the hill was a good defensive position, but it was very exposed to the elements. We eventually found a dry place for the mortar gun and ammunition and then tried to find somewhere to rest our weary bodies, but everywhere felt damp. The best we could find was a small clump of trees and we decided to bed down there. We put our waterproof gas capes over our bodies and tried to rest, but this was difficult in these foul conditions.

We had no hot drink or food that night and I woke repeatedly feeling hungry, thirsty and freezing cold. It seemed like a bad dream with the rainwater cascading off the trees on to my cape. Just after dawn, I heard an engine coming up the track. I looked up and saw that it was the battalion ambulance. When it came to a stop, the medical officer and the padre jumped out of the back. They hadn't been sleeping in the open like us. They had been lying in the dry on stretcher beds in the ambulance. I felt envious. Little did I know that I would soon be taking the padre's place in that blessed ambulance.

The following morning, we moved closer to the front line where, some miles ahead of us, an assault was being made on the German defences on Monte Camino. Our stay here was short as we were soon ordered to retreat to another staging camp in the city of Naples.

On the journey to Naples we passed by the ruins of Pompei at the foot of Mount Vesuvius, stopping only for a few minutes so that we could relieve ourselves. It seemed immensely disrespectful to be using this beautiful ancient site as a public toilet, but we were all desperate after our long, uncomfortable drive! On arrival in the city, we were buoyed up by the news that Badoglio and the Kingdom of Italy had declared war on Nazi Germany. We were still hoping that the Germans would turn tail and that we would not be called upon to fight. However, we were aware that unless these things changed soon, this was probably our last stop before we joined our battalion on the front line.

We arrived in Naples not long after the Germans had evacuated. The city was in chaos and as we were directed to our billets, we saw that large parts of Naples were in ruins. There were bombed buildings everywhere and tap water, electricity and gas were unavailable in most districts. The sewerage system had been largely destroyed and the poor hygienic conditions had led to a spread of typhus and thousands of people were sheltered in the network of ancient tunnels that ran under the city.

Fortunately for us, despite the chaos all around, we found cooking facilities at an old, deserted hotel that was to serve as our billet. At least that meant that we would be fed, but conditions there were not great. An officer popped his head in and told us to sleep on the floor rather than in the beds because they were full of lice.

While we were in Naples, we seemed to spend all our time washing up and cleaning in the kitchens of our billet. It was a tedious time, but in the evening, after the work was over, we all sat in what was once the hotel lounge and sang some of the popular sentimental songs from back home, and a few mournful Irish ballads: 'Danny Boy', 'Galway Bay' and 'The Mountains of Mourne'. Perversely, these baleful singsongs cheered me up considerably.

One day after cleaning the kitchen, a few of us decided to go into the city to try to see what was left of it. Everywhere we went we were confronted by angry women with empty shopping baskets, all chanting just one word, 'Pane, Pane, Pane'. It was obvious that they were desperate for bread to feed their families, and they held us responsible for the shortages and their hunger. It wasn't quite the liberator's welcome that we were hoping for.

Later, we came across an old man lying in the road with his neck resting on a tram rail. He was groaning and uttering the same word: 'Pane, Pane!' He would not budge from his position. By now, a large crowd had gathered urging us to do something. We dragged him very forcefully from the rail to safety and made him sit up on the pavement against a bomb-damaged building. He just scowled and swore at us in Italian. He obviously resented the fact that we had prevented him from ending his misery.

Gradually, we learned all that had been happening here in the previous few weeks. On 13 September as the tide was turning at Salerno, the Germans declared a curfew and a state of siege. They arranged for the following proclamation to appear on the walls of the city under the name of Colonel Walter Schöll:

> With immediate action from today, I assume the absolute control with full powers of the city of Naples and the surrounding areas.
>
> Every single citizen who behaves calmly will enjoy my protection. On the other hand, anyone who openly or surreptitiously acts against the German armed forces will be executed. Moreover, the home of the miscreant and its immediate surroundings will be destroyed and reduced to ruins. Every German soldier wounded or murdered will be avenged a hundred times.
>
> I order a curfew from 8 p.m. to 6 a.m. Only in case of alarm will it be allowed to use the road in order to reach the nearest shelter.
>
> A state of siege is proclaimed. Within 24 hours all weapons and ammunition of any kind, including shotguns, hand grenades, etc., must be surrendered. Anyone who, after that period, is found in possession of a weapon will be immediately executed. The delivery of weapons and ammunition shall be made to the German military patrols. People must keep calm and act reasonably. (*Lewis, 1978*)

On 12 September a sailor who had attacked the German troops was executed in front of a crowd of 600 people. The event was filmed, and the crowd was ordered to applaud the execution. On the same day Schöll, who had organised the public execution, required all men aged 18 to 35 to surrender themselves to the German authorities. Unsurprisingly, of the 3,000 men expected, only 150 showed up. In response, German soldiers arrested over 8,000 men and deported all of them for forced labour.

The arrests were followed by the shooting of eight prisoners of war in via Cesario Console, and a tank opened fire upon students who were beginning to gather in the nearby university. On the same day, 500 men were deported to Teverola, near Caserta, and forced to watch the execution of fourteen policemen, who had offered armed resistance to the occupying forces. On 23 September Colonel Schöll ordered additional measures to suppress the population, including the evacuation of the entire coastal area up 300m from the waterfront to allow the creation of a 'military security zone', prior to the mining of the port.

A further outbreak of fighting occurred in Vomero, where a group of armed Italian men stopped a German car and killed the driver. The same day, fierce fighting followed in different areas of the city between the insurgents and German troops. Meanwhile, a group of Italians moved on the Parco di Capodimonte in response to rumours that Germans were executing prisoners there. Unable to quell the riots and with the Allied armies approaching fast, the Germans decided to evacuate, but not until the city had been destroyed.

Although the capture of Naples had been a key objective of the Allied plan, the Germans made sure that it wasn't much of a prize. Much of the bombing and shelling had been carried out by the Allies, but German demolition teams had done even more damage. Kesselring had been explicit about protecting churches and monasteries, but nothing else was spared. The departing German forces removed or destroyed all communications, water, and power grids. They burned hotels, mined buildings, collapsed bridges and ripped out railway tracks. Ships in the harbour were sunk, adding to those already destroyed. As a result, by the time we arrived nearly 800,000 Neapolitans depended upon the Allies for their basic survival. No wonder they were hungry and begging us for food.

We also discovered that immediately after capturing Naples, the Allies had enlisted the help of the city's top crime family, the Camorra. The family had a Robin Hood image and were ferociously anti-Fascist during Mussolini's reign. The people of Naples both feared and admired them because they were merciless to their enemies, who could be described as anyone who did not do what the Camorra wanted them to do. In exchange for their help, the Camorra crime syndicate received special favours from the Allies and for the rest of the war they ran the black market almost untouched. No wonder the Neapolitans saw us as little better than the Germans.

That night German aircraft dropped bombs in and around the port, but luckily, they didn't come too close to us. In the morning, we were ordered to leave our billet to make way for the men coming along behind us. Our next move was to tented accommodation just a few miles north of the city. On our journey, we came across a German soldier who had been killed while driving his jeep (known as a Kübelwagen). Some callous and cruel soldiers from our side had placed his rigid body on the grass verge at the roadside with his hands still stretched out as if driving an imaginary car. The poor man was frozen in death. I detested this show of barbarism. Were we no better than that? Who could do such a thing to a fellow human being?

What the Allied commanders did not know was that Hitler had met with Rommel and Kesselring to discuss future operations in Italy on 30 September 1943. Rommel had proposed a defensive line north of Rome, while Kesselring had advocated holding a line south of Rome. Hitler preferred Kesselring's recommendation, and he revoked his previous decision to subordinate Kesselring's forces under Rommel's command.

On 19 October, Hitler made Kesselring the overall commander of the forces in Italy.

The Allied commanders were still banking on a German retreat north of Rome and hoped the city would fall in weeks. Their plan was to capture airfields near Rome to ensure air superiority and protect Allied-held airfields in central and southern Italy. However, they were not blind to the fact that an advance on the ground might be difficult, particularly if the Germans chose to defend south of Rome. Alexander remained concerned about whether he had sufficient strength to take on the Germans should they decide to stand and fight. Alexander could no longer count on significant reinforcements nor massive air support, and he feared that still more troops could be withdrawn from Italy for an American plan for an invasion of southern France. Once again, Allied strategy was conflicted and confused.

In mid-October, the Germans had established defensive lines along the Volturno and Trigno rivers. The Volturno was a formidable obstacle, up to 60m wide in places. In the summer it was normally only 1m deep, but it was liable to flood in the late autumn. When it did, it overflowed its banks, which were up to 5m high. Behind this barrier were 35,000 German troops. There was an equally formidable number of German troops opposing the British 8th Army behind the Trigno river.

As we moved north from Naples, we encountered increasingly difficult terrain. The Apennine Mountains form a spine along the back of the Italian 'boot'. In the most mountainous areas of Abruzzo, peaks over 900m stretched across more than half the width. This type of terrain was quite easy to defend and very hard to attack.

On 20 October we arrived at our next campsite outside Teano, about 60km north of Naples. Our billet was just rows of two-man tents. There were few houses here, but right in front of our camp was a huge rock around 60m long by 30m high. It was at Teano that we first caught up with our battalion and the headquarters of B Echelon, where the personnel and vehicles needed to distribute stores and supplies for the troops on the front line were assembled (See Plate 18).

On 27 October 1943 troops from our regiment took part in a successful attack on the hills in the Calvi Risorta area. This was followed by further actions at Gloriana and Roccamonfina. This was all some distance from Teano. There was nothing for us to do at our campsite except keep our Bren gun carrier clean and our mortar and ammunition dry. We had plenty of time to think about what might be in store for us.

One morning, while on parade, they asked for volunteers to make up a carrying party for the battalion fighting in the front line at a place called Calabritto. We were told it was no easy task, but men were urgently needed to carry supplies up to our men who were becoming weary and worn down by the constant German attacks. Having become increasingly bored, about twenty of us volunteered.

The next morning, I boarded a Bren gun carrier with three of my mates and followed a 3-ton lorry full of supplies. After travelling some way on our journey, I heard a rumble that sounded like thunder in the distance, but it soon became apparent that this wasn't thunder, it was the roar of heavy gunfire and mortar shelling. At last, we came abreast of the line of heavy guns and could see ours[36] sited both sides of the road and in an extended line across the fields. They were blazing away at targets miles away. The noise had been bearable as we approached, but now it was thunderous as we passed by the gun muzzles.

At length we arrived at 'A' Echelon. This was the staging place for reinforcements for the battalion as well as being a forward store of ammunition, food and water for the companies in the front line. 'A' Echelon was situated on high ground covered with edible chestnut trees behind the village of Roccamonfina. Our task was to take supplies from 'A' Echelon to the rifle companies on the front line to avoid the need for them to leave their positions. Ominously, the sergeant told us:

> Where you are going, you will find most of the men in their slit trenches. Unfortunately, you will be on open ground, and in the event of an attack there, you must find whatever cover is available to you. (*Vere, 2006*)

After we had loaded up the Bren gun carrier, we passed through Roccamonfina and drove out into open countryside along a tree-lined road until we came to a Bailey bridge[37] across a gorge. An air battle was still going on overhead. We crossed over the bridge and continued to the village of Saraceri. This was a place that we had been to some weeks before, but we were told that the village had changed hands several times since then and had been reoccupied by the Germans just days before.

However, we found Saraceri empty, and we made our own billets in a deserted house. We had been warned not to make any noise or have fires that would generate flames and smoke that would draw attention. An NCO stressed to us to always keep a low profile in daylight hours

36 These guns were Ordnance QF 25-pounders that were the most widely used British field gun used during the Second World War.

37 A Bailey bridge is a type of portable, prefabricated bridge made of wood and steel components that were small and light enough to be carried in trucks and lifted into place by hand, without the use of a crane. However, these bridges were strong enough to carry tanks.

because there were snipers and machine gunners all around. We didn't feel particularly safe here and decided that Saraceri was as far as we could go in the Bren gun carrier, so we parked it up under some trees and camouflaged it as best we could with the intention of continuing our journey on foot. The stores were heavy, and we had some distance still to travel up to the front-line battalion, but we had been told we should only make this final leg under the cover of darkness and in complete silence.

We started off from the village at around 10 p.m. by the light of the early winter moon. As we walked along a mountain path, we came to a wall running along the side of us. In a niche in the wall there was a roadside shrine containing a statue of the Madonna. It seemed so incongruous to see those sad eyes that had last gazed down upon me a lifetime ago in Corpus Christi church.

We managed to deliver the supplies to the front-line battalion without incident. All was quiet and there was no gunfire while we were there. Having done our job, we made our way back to Saraceri and when we found the Bren gun carrier, thankfully undiscovered, we turned in for some sleep. In the early hours of morning, just before dawn, we returned to 'B' Echelon in our carrier.

Carrying parties were arranged for every night that week and some of these were more hazardous than others. One night, the Germans made an attack on our front line from their positions under the foot of the mountain and almost succeeded in overrunning it. During the German attack, they constantly called out each other's Christian names, making sure that their comrades were safe. It was very disturbing to think that these men who were trying to kill us were so close by. We never stayed around long after we had delivered our supplies and always scooted back to Saraceri as fast as we could manage it. However, this is not to say that Saraceri was safe. On some days, mortar bombs fell in and around the village, and we often heard the thuds and saw plumes of smoke and steam rising from the ground in front of us where the mortar bombs had fallen. Thankfully, these all fell short of our positions, presumably because we were just too far out of range.

However, it was obvious to all of us that our boys were having a bad time at Calabritto as the stream of casualties being brought back to the field hospital at 'B' Echelon was increasing. One young officer, who had only just joined us, was killed on his first evening with the battalion. Fortunately, on 8 November the order came down for us to pause and regroup.

The winter rains that had started at the end of September had been relentless, making roads and passes extremely difficult and turning the open country into a sea of mud. Many of our men who had been on the front line for weeks were now suffering from severe exhaustion. The order to retreat came only just in time.

My comrades in the Royal Berkshire Regiment's 10th Battalion were still withdrawing from the mountains at Calabritto when I received orders to take a carrier to assist with the retreat to the 'B' Echelon base HQ. This was on the morning of 10 November. I had seen and heard the German heavy guns and mortars firing all through the night before and it brought home the realisation that the enemy was now very close indeed and seemed to be getting closer.

We bumped along up the track through woods with shattered trees, shell holes and slit trenches, and through small, ruined villages now swarming with Allied troops. A badly shelled house had fallen in the road behind us and there were recently dug Allied and German graves with neat white wooden crosses all along the roadside.

On climbing one of the many peaks, I stopped to look down on the wide sunlit plain stretching down to the sea that was now firmly in enemy hands. A hastily erected notice in English was posted to a tree reading: 'Don't stop you are under Enemy Observation'. This rather took my mind off the view so I raced along. Soon there was no further sign of Allied troops and for a second time in my military career a British military policeman popped out of nowhere and shouted: 'Stop! Stop. The Germans are just round that bend.' Had the man not risked his own life to warn me, we could have been killed in a matter of moments. I stopped the carrier, undecided whether to find another route down from the peak, or to return the way I had come.

Fearing the reaction if I returned having achieved nothing, I decided to carry on. I stepped on the accelerator and pointed in the direction of what appeared to be a reasonable mule track down the mountainside. As I accelerated down the bumpy track I heard a dull thud of a German mortar on my right. The shriek of shrapnel whizzing through the air above my head was truly terrifying. I drove on frantically, very conscious that I was, no doubt, in the 'beaten zone' of a German mortar crew somewhere up on the hill.

A short distance further and I rounded a corner and gained another view of Monte Camino, the most important part of the German front line. The mountain had about seven distinct ridges and it seemed to me that it was nothing but crags and precipices. This was where our boys had been fighting. The only way ahead now was a mule track up the centre.

Monte Camino was a natural fortress with its caves and huge rocks providing protection to the snipers, mortars and machine guns of the

German troops sheltering there. We had been told previously that the German machine guns could fire 900 rounds a minute, which was not a comforting thought as I drove over open ground. The mountain guarded the road north, and on the other side was a vast plain that provided excellent positions for tanks and artillery.

Turning a corner, I met the first string of Allied troops who were being led back towards the road. They had clearly suffered considerable hardships through exposure to the unpleasant weather and enemy fire. Some of them had been up there for five days, some for ten. I picked up two men who you might term 'walking wounded' who would not have made it back without help. Despite their exhaustion and their wounds, they told me about hand-to-hand fighting and how they had killed German soldiers with rifles, grenades, bayonets, pistols and knives. These conversations troubled me. Far from being battle-weary they seemed to relish the killing, almost as if they couldn't wait to get back to it. How was it possible that good and honest men like these had become so immune to the barbarism of war? They seemed proud of the fact that they were killing machines, capable of cutting another man's throat or throwing a grenade into a dugout, maiming and killing with a single action. Why did they have so much hate? They then told of how they had seen their friends and comrades blown apart and maimed at German hands and the cause of their hatred became understandable. Not for the first time, the thought troubled me that maybe one day soon I would develop such hatred for my fellow man.

The withdrawal of our troops was completed that night. Thankfully, we made it back to 'B' Echelon before the heavy rains began, and we took some comfort in the heavy barrage of protective fire put up by our artillery. However, the noise made sleep impossible. It wasn't just the noise of the guns, but also the sound of lorries, carriers and marching feet and voices as the men continued to come down that dreadful mule track, tired, worn down and dehumanised by their experiences. I looked out from our tent, and I shall never forget their drawn, dirty, bearded faces as they plodded through the mud.

As the US war correspondent Ernie Pyle wrote at the time:

> No one who had not seen that mud, those dark skies, those forbidding ridges and ghostlike clouds that unveiled and then quickly hid the enemy had the right to be impatient with the progress along the road to Rome. (*Adelman, 1968*)

In the morning, we were ordered to move out. I started up the carrier and headed back to a deserted Italian village, where we were told that we should stop and await further orders. During that period most of the talk among the men from the front line was about Monte Camino, at first in the past tense, and then in anxious anticipation as their thoughts turned to the fact that a fresh assault was being planned.

For a second night, none of us got much sleep as our artillery put up a terrific barrage on the mountain. We spent most of the night chatting and gazing across the plain as hundreds of tracer shells flew over our heads. Higher up on the slopes there were flashes as the shells and explosives landed and soon the whole mountain was obscured in smoke.

It was still pouring with rain in the morning, and it was impossible to keep dry as water came streaming through the holes under the armpits of the capes. We moved into another deserted village, where we stayed the whole of the next day and managed to get our things dry before large wood fires overnight. Meanwhile, other units were commencing an attack up the mountain slopes, and we were called forward to make a mortar attack on the slope of Monte Camino.

Although we were in good heart, rations and ammunition were low and we were pinned down by two machine gun positions that were well dug in: one on the south side and one on north side of the road. Early in the morning of 13 November 1943 we dug our own trench and had barely completed the task when the Germans launched a mortar attack of their own.

It was by the side of a mule track on this treacherous and precipitous mountainside that I took a hit from a German shell while setting up our mortar. The date – Friday 13 November – is etched forever in my memory. It was exactly one year to the day that I had (reluctantly) joined the Army.

The last thing that I remember was the rattle of small stones on my helmet, but then I immediately felt the warm blood pouring from my legs, groin and arms. My mind rapidly explored every part of my body. I had been hit by multiple pieces of red-hot shrapnel from an exploding mortar shell. I passed out in unbearable agony.

Because of our position, no medical assistance could be offered where I lay but at precisely 7 a.m. on 13 November, I was picked up by a stretcher chain[38] and carried to the Advanced Dressing Station from No. 10 Field Surgical Unit (FSU). I was completely unaware of the fate

38 A stretcher chain in the Monte Camino range reached over three mountains and was made up by about 1,000 men (Indian, British, Italian). They were spread out four to a stretcher with varying distances between each team according to the difficulty of terrain. Each group brought a loaded stretcher anything from 50m to 250m each and handed it over to the next group and took an empty one back with them.

of my crew mates and to this day I do not know whether they lived or died. I thought about this a good deal in later life and realised that I might well be able to find out about them if I tried, but something stopped me. For many years I couldn't bring myself to look back on that day.

The tank warfare in the Western Desert in North Africa in 1940–43 had proven the need for surgical teams that could function close to the fighting and move between larger medical units 'in an ever-changing pattern depending on the tactical situation'. (*Crew, 1956*) Because evacuation by air was impossible in the Italian campaign, there was no alternative but to treat the wounded close to the front line.

The Advanced Dressing Station operated from a large Bedford truck,[39] which carried an operating table, lighting equipment, instruments, drums and sterile dressings. I read later that one of the lessons learned in the Great War was that it was essential that medical units were mobile so that patients could be classified and prioritised as soon as possible based on an immediate assessment of their chances of surviving their wounds. Casualties were grouped as:

- requiring resuscitation before any surgery or evacuation,
- requiring immediate operation and holding until fit to move,
- fit for evacuation.

This assessment was carried out in the back of this truck, and I was classified as being in the second category. That is, requiring an immediate operation. It was then that I was moved to the FSU. I knew little about it at the time, but this FSU had beds for forty casualties, and was manned by a surgeon, an anaesthetist, and five medical orderlies. One medical orderly was a corporal who had received the training to make himself useful in the operating theatre, the other was a lance corporal who could type. It made perfect sense when it was explained to me later that the ability to type was a most important asset given the importance of capturing accurate, contemporaneous, medical notes.

The condition of the FSU's generator and the lighting was of critical importance. Each operation took an hour on average, and because so many soldiers had multiple wounds, a surgical team could deal with no more than twelve to sixteen such cases in twenty-four hours. It was incumbent on the surgeon, therefore, to make rapid decisions and avoid

39 A Bedford MW, a 15 cwt 4x2 truck.

'unnecessary or hopeless' operations. It was the established practice not to waste energy by operating on patients who were unlikely to survive or who were capable of being evacuated. Indeed, most surgeons agreed that it was less hazardous to evacuate a wounded man than to operate in the FSU.

On arrival at the FSU, I was rushed into the penthouse operating theatre, which was a grand name for canvas draped over poles extending backwards from a truck. It had a particularly good lighting system with a spotlight and a 1 kilowatt generator and some dozen or more bulbs mounted on an overhead wooden trellis. The surgeon in charge of this operating theatre was Major Arthur Bullough of the RAMC.[40]

I had lost too much blood to be aware of my surroundings but after a short while Arthur Bullough terminated the operation, having decided that I had a better chance of survival if I was evacuated rather than operated on there. The medical team then set about making my wounds safe to travel so that I could be evacuated as soon as possible. The team cleaned my wounds of foreign bodies, removed dead tissue, controlled bleeding by tying off my damaged larger blood vessels, and relieved tension in my leg and arm. They left the shrapnel that they couldn't get to easily (and I lived with it in my body ever after).

After the medical team had done their best, I was moved by ambulance to the Casualty Clearing Station (CCS), which lay further back from the battlefield. Although I was drifting in and out of consciousness, I distinctly remember the ambulance driver shouting: 'Get out of the way, I've got a dying man in here!'

After a long, bumpy and uncomfortable journey we arrived eventually at the CCS, which had its own surgical team and 200 beds. Despite its distance from the front line, it seemed to me that the CCS was being used by the enemy gunners for range-finding. While I lay there barely conscious and in immense pain, a shell burst in the air immediately above my tent.

After they had resuscitated me, most of my blood-stained clothing was removed before I was taken to the operating theatre. The skin of my leg and groin was then cleaned with soap and water and my whole leg was shaved, while my wounds were protected with a dressing.

---

40 Arthur Stanley Bullough (15 January 1910 to 10 September 2000) was born in Hindley, near Wigan, and qualified from Manchester University in 1934. After junior posts, he joined the RAMC and was given command of No. 10 Field Surgical Unit. After the war, he returned to Manchester and served as a consultant surgeon.

An antiseptic lotion was then wiped over me. This was incredibly painful, but the CCS surgeon explained that he regarded skin as extremely valuable and aimed to conserve it if there was the slightest chance that it might still be viable. The edges of my wounds to my arm and legs were then trimmed with a scalpel and the entry wound on my thigh was extended to expose the underlying fascia that connected my skin to the underlying tissue. The damaged fascia was then cut and split further both sideways and long ways. Because my muscles did not respond to pinching and did not bleed when cut, they were cut out of my leg.

A haematoma over the other side of my thigh was then cut out and drained of blood, and more jagged shrapnel was removed from the injured muscle from my leg and groin. Once the bleeding slowed the wounds were not closed but were left open to the air.

Four days later, penicillin and sulphonamide powder were applied to my wounds, with Vaseline gauze, dry dressing and wool, and the dressings were made tight. Because none of my bones were fractured, these dressings were secured by adhesive strapping. Although the medical staff worked at great speed for obvious reasons, they never sacrificed proper care. They had learned through experience that the value of their work was lost if dressings were carelessly applied so that they came off in transit when the patient moved.

Despite all the best efforts of the CCS medical team, I was still in a bad way and at 8:30 p.m. on 14 November, I suffered a sudden severe haemorrhage after my femoral artery was exposed. The bleeding was eventually controlled by clips applied by the RAMC surgeon, Brian Truscott[41] but my condition was now critical, and Truscott gave me the devastating news that my right leg would have to be amputated from high above my knee.

The operation commenced at 10.30 p.m. on 16 November 1943. The amputation was performed by Truscott in No. 9 FSU Unit (14 CCS). That man undoubtedly saved my life that night.

After the operation I was treated with diazine,[42] and placed in a bed on high blocks for the next twelve hours. The high blocks were used to enable the physiotherapists to perform targeted exercises to strengthen the muscles around what remained of my leg.

41 Brian McNeill Truscott qualified as a doctor in 1935 and became expert in abdominal surgery. On the outbreak of war in 1939 he joined the RAMC and saw active service in North Africa, Salerno, Anzio, and in northern Europe. He attained the rank of lieutenant colonel and was appointed MBE in recognition of his war service.

42 An antibiotic used in cases of urinary tract infection.

Five days later, on 21 November 1943, I was moved to 92 General Hospital and later to 67 General Hospital in the Cavalry Barracks at Naples. I had never felt so miserable and in so much pain: I thought that my life was over.

While I lay there in hospital in Naples, thinking that things could get no worse, I was brought the awful news that my elder brother, Jimmy, had been killed in action. I found out later that my mother had been informed of the seriousness of my wounds and when she received a second telegram, she assumed that it was informing her of my death. Imagine her horror and despair in finding out that she had lost another much-loved son.

Jimmy was not like me. He had volunteered willingly for the Royal Navy in 1940 when he was 21 and had been posted to the Seaman and Communicators branch at Chatham, where he trained as a telegraph operator. He looked so dapper and handsome when he came home on leave wearing his Navy uniform.

Most of the telegraphists, or 'sparkers' as they were called, had worked in the Post Office before the war, but Jimmy had no previous involvement in telegraphy. However, he was a fast learner and could soon send Morse code messages at the required speed of twenty-two words a minute. As an ordinary telegraphist, Jimmy was responsible for keeping a constant watch for Morse code or speech radio messages on board HMS *Santa,* an Antarctic whaler that had been converted for minesweeping duties. Whalers were particularly suited for minesweeping because they were robust boats designed to work in all types of weather and had large, clear working decks.

HMS *Santa* had been part of a flotilla of minesweepers that had been deployed to the Strait of Bonifacio between Corsica and Sardinia in October 1943. The requirement for shallow-draft minesweepers had been recognised following the loss of HMS *Cromarty* in the Straits of Bonifacio on 23 October 1943. This was put down to the ship's design.

Unfortunately, the shallower berth was no insurance against contact mines, and HMS *Santa* was sunk outside the port of Maddalena in Sicily on 23 November 1943. Maddalena had been an important base for the Italian Navy and was of significant strategic importance to the Allies. As such it had been heavily mined and Allied minesweepers faced the constant threat of air and sea attack from German forces on the Italian west coast. HMS *Santa* had the critical but perilous job of keeping the supply lines open to the 5th Army in which I was serving.

We'll never know precisely what happened to HMS *Santa* but it is thought that it was sunk after it hit one of the 405 defensive contact mines that had been laid by the German minelayers *Brandenburg* and

Pommern on 26 August 1943. These mines were tethered at the end of a cable just below the surface of the water. The mines were spread thinly, to create an impression of minefields existing across large areas so that a single mine inserted strategically on a shipping route could stop maritime movements for days while the entire area was swept.

Jimmy died with all twenty-two members of the crew and the Commander, Lt James Leslie Everett, who had only just taken over the command. They are all commemorated now on the Royal Naval memorial on Plymouth Hoe.

After several weeks – I'm not sure how many – I had recovered sufficiently to be transferred back to England. Captain Thomas Sibbald, RAMC, authorised my evacuation on the hospital ship *Llandovery Castle*[43] on 29 January 1944.

---

43 SS *Llandovery Castle* made her maiden trip on 25 September 1925 and was requisitioned as a hospital ship in the Second World War. After the war it served as a cruise ship with the Union Castle Line African lines until 1953.

Chapter 18

ANZIO AND CASSINO

Meanwhile, the Italian campaign continued. The drive north was not easy for Allied troops. In the east the Canadians tried to breach the German defensive line at the coastal town of Ortona on the Adriatic Sea. Ortona was not previously considered to be strategically important, but the bay was deep, and the Allies were keen to take Ortona and make use of it as a port.

When the Germans realised the importance that the Allies had attached to Ortona, they moved two elite battalions to protect the town. They also began blowing up buildings to create piles of rubble, from which they set up fight positions and laid down mines throughout the town. The house-to-house fighting was so intense that the battle became referred to as the 'Italian Stalingrad'. (*Battistelli, 2023*) The Canadians succeeded eventually, but only at great cost.

In the west, the advance had ground to a halt with the onset of winter blizzards at the end of December, making close air support and movement almost impossible. The only viable routes from Naples to Rome were Highway 6 (the Via Casilina), which was dominated to the south by Monte Cassino, and Highway 7 (the old Roman Appian Way), which followed the west coast but ran into the Pontine Marshes south of Rome, which the Germans had flooded.

The peaks of the hills surrounding Cassino allowed the German defenders to detect Allied movement and direct highly accurate artillery fire, which slowed down any northward advance along Highway 6. Because of the historical significance of the abbey at Cassino, Kesselring had ordered German units not to include it in their defensive positions and informed the Vatican and the Allies accordingly in December 1943. Despite this, some Allied reconnaissance aircraft maintained they could see German troops inside the monastery and the Allied commanders agreed that in order to capture Rome, Cassino would have to be taken first.

Mark Clark's plan was for the British (under Lieutenant General Richard McCreery) to advance north across the confluence of the Gari and Liri rivers on 17 January 1944 in support of the main attack by American troops, under Major General Geoffrey Keyes, across the Gari river (also known as the Rapido), 8km downstream of Cassino. The main thrust would commence on 20 January. At the same time, French troops led by General Alphonse Juin would make a 'right hook' move towards Monte Cairo, the main peak of an isolated mountain range that extends east for about 16–18km from the road from Rome to Naples.

Clark did not believe there was much chance of an early breakthrough, but he felt that the attacks would draw German reserves away from Rome. He had already decided that it was essential for political and psychological reasons that the US 5th Army should capture Rome prior to the invasion of France. He decided that an amphibious landing in January at the Italian coastal town of Anzio would make this possible.

Just before Christmas 1943, Churchill had become re-enthused about the Italian campaign and according to Clark he assumed a role 'as a sort of super commander in chief, a role that he loved to play'. (*Clark, 1954*)

Eisenhower and Alexander were summoned to Carthage in Tunis, where Churchill was recovering from a bout of pneumonia.[44] On Christmas Day the Allied leaders met the British Prime Minister to discuss the situation. Throughout the conference Churchill wore his padded silk dressing gown with gold and blue Chinese dragons, while the commanders wore their respective uniforms. The fact that he was allowed to dictate strategy is a mark of the vigour and determination of the man, but it also illustrates the extent to which he was above challenge. He was hell-bent on getting his way regarding an invasion and dismissed all objections about supplies and reinforcements and whether German strength and determination had been underestimated.

After their conference, Alexander sent Clark a message:

> Certain decisions were definitely reached today at a high-level conference. Operation Shingle [Anzio] is to be strengthened and will be put into effect at end of January. We will have available 88 LSTs which will permit mounting of an amphibious operation of more

44 He had been diagnosed with left lower lobe pneumonia and two episodes of atrial fibrillation. He had been prescribed sulphadiazine and digitalis leaf by Lord Moran, his personal physician.

than two divisions. If you desire to use two American divisions, I will replace them by transferring two 8th Army divisions to X Corps of 5th Army. Start planning straightaway. (*Gilbert, Churchill and America, 2005*)

Clark welcomed the decision, and he hoped that the Anzio landing (code-named *Operation Shingle*) would threaten German supply lines and might force the German commanders to withdraw to positions north of Rome.

On 27 December, Churchill made a five-hour flight from Carthage to Marrakesh, using an oxygen regulator as the plane rose to 12,000ft to cross the mountains. From the airport he was driven to the Villa Taylor, where he and Roosevelt had met one year before. From there he telegraphed to Roosevelt that he was living 'in the lap of luxury, thanks to overflowing American hospitality'. He was also delighted that the Americans had agreed to the Anzio landings. 'I thank God for this fine decision which engages us once again in whole-hearted unity upon a great enterprise.' (*Gilbert, Churchill and America, 2005*)

Alexander told the American general John Lucas that Shingle 'would astonish the world and make the invasion of France unnecessary'. However, the risks were well understood. It was agreed that the British 5th Division should be put under Clark's command so that the hazards were shared to offset any criticism at home if things went badly. However, Churchill had no self-doubt. His primary concern was concerned about who would get the credit for the operation. He pointed out that he and Alexander had been responsible for the whole planning and control of the whole thing and wrote: 'It will lead to bitterness in Great Britain when the claim is stridently put forward, as it surely will be, that 'the Americans have taken Rome.' (*Trevelyan, 1981*)

The American general John P. Lucas was given responsibility for the landings and beachhead. According to Alexander, he was 'the best American corps commander'. (*Trevelyan, 1981*). Lucas, who was nicknamed 'Foxy Grandpa' or 'Corncob Charlie', because of his pipe did not share Churchill's confidence or enthusiasm. He was further dismayed when a rehearsal for *Operation Shingle* went disastrously wrong and forty small amphibious transport vehicles were lost.

When the American and British planners met at Marrakesh on 7 January 1944, they proposed that the operation should be postponed, allowing time for one more amphibious rehearsal. Churchill would have none of it. He insisted that well-trained troops required no such preparations. Even though the Royal Navy remained pessimistic about both the winter weather and the continued maintenance of the beachhead after the initial landing, Churchill reported to President Roosevelt on 8 January that a unanimous agreement had been reached in favour of a reinforced two-division assault at Anzio on 22 January.

Alexander confirmed to Clark that the Prime Minister's passion for an early operation outweighed any concerns about the comparative weakness of the assault. The fatal parallels between Anzio and Gallipoli were complete.

Meanwhile, British troops had forced a crossing of the Garigliano river on 17 January, but the Allies failed to appreciate the frailty of the German position and, rather than pressing on, they hesitated, allowing time for Kesselring to bring in two divisions of reinforcements on 21 January and they stabilised the German position. The British sustained some 4,000 casualties during the period of the first battle.

The central thrust by the US troops commenced three hours after sunset on 20 January, but the lack of time to prepare meant that the approach to the Garigliano river was still hazardous due to uncleared mines and booby traps. Although some troops were able to get across, the shortage of amphibious vehicles following the disastrous rehearsal for *Operation Shingle* made the crossing problematic. The troops who did make it across were isolated with no armoured support, and they were left highly vulnerable to German counterattacks by tanks and self-propelled guns.

The Americans were forced back across the Gari river by mid-morning of 21 January. They renewed their attack but there was still no armoured support, and they were hit hard when daylight came the next day. The assault had been a costly failure, with the loss of 2,100 Allied soldiers.

Clark criticised Major General Fred L. Walker's execution of the battle plan. Walker responded that the entire battle had been foolhardy and unnecessary, and that Clark's plan was guaranteed to fail. The battle was one of the largest defeats suffered by the US Army during the Second World War and was the subject of an investigation in 1946 by the US Congress to establish responsibility for the disaster. Once again, no one was at fault; no one was to blame.

The first landings at Anzio took place on the clear moonlit night of 22 January under a starry sky and a gentle breeze. The huge convoy that set sail from Naples met with little German resistance and the beach commander, John Lucas, began to feel more confident. He wrote in his diary:

> I think we have a good chance of making a killing. I have many misgivings but am also optimistic. I struggle to be calm and collected and fortunately am associating with naval officers whom I don't know very well which takes my mind off things. (*Hamilton, 2011*)

Immediately prior to the landings, Royal Navy ships had pounded the shore with rockets containing 13kg of TNT. The noise was deafening, but there was no answering fire from the Germans. It appeared that, unlike at Salerno, the Germans had been caught off-guard as the Allied troops poured ashore largely untroubled.[45]

The unopposed landing gave Lucas the opportunity to break out from the beachhead and cut off the German supply lines, leaving the way open to Rome. However, he failed to seize the opportunity, deciding instead to wait until all his ground troops had landed and the beachhead had been fully secured. The BBC correspondent Wynford Vaughan-Thomas wrote to his colleague Denis Johnston:

> It is just normal military fuck-up with an American accent. We are commanded by a dear old pussy-cat who purrs away, that we are all happy on the beachhead, and in a sense we are. (*Trevelyan, 1981*)

Churchill, intervening from many miles away, took out his frustration on Alexander, as Alexander confirmed in his memoirs:

> Of the many messages I received from Winston Churchill ... the first reached me during a lull and ran something like this: What are you doing sitting down doing nothing? Why don't you use your armour in a great scythe-like movement through the mountains? (*North, 1962*)

It was not until 30 January – some eight days after the landing – that Lucas ordered the British and American troops to advance on Cisterna and Campoleone. It was too late. Kesselring had moved troops to the beachhead and by 31 January 1944 eight German divisions had it surrounded.

The Allies had not realised that Kesselring's strategy was based on delaying the Allies to provide time to prepare the German defensive line, where they intended to stand firm. Fighting through driving rain, deep mud, bitter winds and snowdrifts, many soldiers contracted trench foot while others fell victim to frostbite. As a result of stubborn

---

45 The supervisor of the landings at the beachhead was Major Dennis Healey, who later became a Labour politician and Chancellor of the Exchequer.

German resistance, the US 5th Army did not breach the German defences until 15 January, having taken six weeks of heavy fighting to advance the last 11km through one of Italy's worst winters in decades. During this time, the Allies sustained 16,000 casualties.

The next attack across the confluence of the Gari river was launched on 24 January, when US and Moroccan French colonial troops launched an assault across the flooded valley north of Cassino. The US troops hardly had time to prepare the new assault, let alone take the rest that they really needed after three months of fighting. The plan was that they would advance into the mountains behind Cassino and would then turn to the left and attack Monte Cassino from high ground. However, the flooding made the approaches exceedingly difficult. Armoured vehicles could only move on paths laid with steel matting and it took eight days of fighting to establish a foothold in the mountains.

On the right, the Moroccan French troops made satisfactory progress initially and General Juin was convinced that Cassino could be bypassed. However, his request for reserves to maintain the momentum of his advance was refused and by 31 January his troops had come to a halt. In the battles, the two Moroccan French divisions sustained 2,500 casualties.

It then became the task of the US troops to fight along the line of hills towards Monte Cassino. The plan was that they could take Cassino and then break down into the Liri valley behind the German defences. However, it was very tough going. The mountains were strewn with boulders and cut through by ravines. Digging foxholes on the rocky ground was impossible and the flatter ground was exposed to constant fire from German positions in the surrounding hills. The ravines provided no sanctuary because they were filled with gorse bushes and barbed wire, while some had also been booby-trapped with mines. The Germans had had three months to prepare their defences, and they had used dynamite to create new positions where they could stockpile ammunition and stores. To top it all, the weather was wet and freezing cold.

By early February, American infantry had managed to capture a strategic point near the small town of San Onofrio, 1.6km from Monte Cassino monastery, and by 7 February a battalion had reached within 400m of the Monte Cassino monastery walls. An American squad even managed to get right up against the walls, with the monks watching the exchange of fire below them. However, attempts to take Monte Cassino were stopped by overwhelming machine gun fire from the slopes below the monastery.

On 11 February, after a final unsuccessful three-day assault on the monastery, the Americans were withdrawn, exhausted and demoralised after two and a half weeks of solid fighting. They had suffered 2,200 casualties. However, the Germans were not having things all their own way. At the height of the battle the Germans had been so concerned about their losses that their commander had requested permission to retreat to a position north of the Anzio bridgehead, but Kesselring refused.

The American units that were withdrawn were replaced by New Zealand troops commanded by Lieutenant General Sir Bernard Freyberg. He was a stocky, rugged soldier who had won the Victoria Cross in the Great War. Indeed, he had been wounded so many times in action that Winston Churchill dubbed him 'the Empire's Salamander'. (*North, 1962*)

Freyberg's plan was a continuation of the first battle: an attack from the north along the mountain ridges followed by an advance from the south-east along the railway line to capture the Cassino railway station, which stood 1.6km south of Cassino town. Freyberg hoped that this would squeeze the Germans out of Cassino town and open the Liri valley. However, he was realistic about the chances of success, which he estimated as only around 50–50, given all the circumstances.

Allied officers became increasingly obsessed with the monastery of Monte Cassino, which they believed was being used by German artillery. Based on unsubstantiated reports from Allied intelligence, the British and American press wrote about German observation posts and artillery positions inside the abbey. Some senior officers reported that they had seen a radio mast when they made a reconnaissance flight. They also reported seeing German uniforms hanging on a clothes line in the abbey courtyard and machine gun emplacements within the walls. However, doubts remained and when the US commander Geoffrey Keyes flew over the monastery he reported that he had seen no evidence of military occupation. When told that other officers had seen enemy troops there, he replied: 'They've been looking so long they're seeing things.' (*Clark, 1954*)

Major General Francis Tuker, whose 4th Indian Division would have the task of attacking the monastery, had made his own appraisal of the situation. In a memorandum to Freyberg, he concluded that regardless of whether the monastery was currently occupied by the Germans, it should be demolished to prevent its occupation in future. Tuker told Mark Clark that he could not attack Cassino until the monastery was destroyed and pointed out that with masonry walls 46m high and 3m thick, bombing with high-capacity bombs would be the only solution.

Alexander asked the US Air Force commander John Cannon whether the USAF was up to the job, and he answered: 'If you let me use the whole of our bomber force against Cassino, we will whip it out like a dead tooth.' (*Smith, 1975*)

Freyberg became convinced that it did not matter whether the monastery was being used as an observation point or not. It would not be difficult for the Germans to bring troops into the monastery if they wanted to. Even if it wasn't occupied today, it might well be tomorrow. All the ground commanders agreed that the monastery needed to be destroyed.

Based on their advice, Eisenhower issued the following order:

> We are fighting in a country ... rich in monuments which illustrate the growth of the civilization which is ours. We are bound to respect those monuments so far as war allows. If we have to choose between destroying a famous building and sacrificing our own men, then our men's lives count infinitely more, and the buildings must go. (*Richardson, 1984*)

Meanwhile, Mark Clark was still preoccupied with the difficulties that the US troops were suffering at the Anzio beachhead. The Germans had now deployed six divisions in a full-scale counterattack to push the British and Americans back into the sea. Blaming Lucas[46] for his decision not to break out of the beachhead sooner, Clark relieved him of his command on 22 February 1944 and replaced him with Lucian K. Truscott. Truscott was a quite different man to Lucas. He was a no-nonsense, Southern redneck with deep-set grey eyes. The British commanders nicknamed him 'Old Gravel mouth'. (*Prefer, 2019*)

Lucas was aggrieved. He had never agreed with the plans for *Operation Shingle* in the first place. He had always argued that he had too few men and that hopes were too high. He placed most of the blame on Churchill, and expressed frustration at:

> The ignorance of war displayed by leaders of people who have been at war for so many years. Shingle had the strong odour of Gallipoli and apparently the same amateur on the coach's bench. Another week might save dozens of lives. But the order comes from a civilian minister of another nation who is impatient of such details and brushes them aside ... The real reasons cannot be military. (*Trevelyan, 1981*)

46 Although bitter towards Clark and the British, who he believed had used him as a scapegoat, Lucas's achievements during the fighting in Italy were recognised with the award of the Army Distinguished Service Medal, the Navy Distinguished Service Medal and the Silver Star.

Lucas was also bitter towards Clark. After all it had been Clark who had warned him: 'Don't stick your neck out, Johnny, like I did at Salerno and got into trouble.' (*Trevelyan, 1981*)

The reality was that Lucas had had too few troops to push on to Rome, and that even if he had broken out of the beachhead, the Allied troops would not have got far given the strength of German defensive forces. What Lucas did was not fundamentally wrong, but his style of command was such that he was easy to blame. Behind the scenes, Churchill was exerting pressure to obtain results from Anzio and Lucas was a ready-made scapegoat.

Inland, the Allies were making slow progress up the Apennines. Instead of a campaign of speed, the Allies had got bogged down in a simple war of attrition. As Churchill rued later: 'I had hoped we were hurling a wildcat on to the shore, but all we got was a beached whale.' (*Allen, 1978*)

In his war diaries, Alan Brooke placed the blame on Mark Clark. He asserted that Clark was too timid in his approach, but it is not obvious what more he could have done. Perhaps the blame should rest more heavily on the man who dreamed up the strategy and who bulldozed it through against the advice of the experts.

On 11 February 1944 Tuker repeated his request for the bombing of the monastery at Monte Cassino. Freyberg passed on his request to Clark on 12 February, requesting fighter-bombers armed with 1,000lb bombs, but Clark and his chief of staff remained unconvinced of the 'military necessity'. (*Reynolds, 1988*)

Brigadier General J.A. Butler, deputy commander of the American 34th Division, said, 'I don't know, but I don't believe the enemy is in the convent. All the fire has been from the slopes of the hill below the wall.' (*Richardson, 1984*) Clark, who was equally unconvinced and still focussed on Anzio, decided to defer the decision to Alexander. After the war, Clark excused himself from any responsibility, writing: 'I said, "You give me a direct order and we'll do it," and he did.' (*Clark, 1954*)

The bombing mission on the morning of 15 February 1944 involved 142 B-17 Flying Fortress heavy bombers, followed by forty-seven B-25 Mitchell and forty B-26 Marauder medium bombers. In all, they dropped 1,150 tonnes of high explosives and incendiary bombs, reducing the monastery on Monte Cassino to rubble. Between bomb runs, Allied artillery pounded the mountain and Allied soldiers, and war correspondents cheered as they looked on.

Clark was not among them. He was staying at the American headquarters at Provenzano, 27km from Monte Cassino. However, even there he could not escape the bombs. Some sixteen of them hit the 5th Army compound, where he was doing paperwork at his desk. He wrote:

> I tried not to pay much attention to anything that wasn't on my desk, but I suppose I was unconsciously listening all the time; and when the clock got around to nine-thirty, I immediately heard the first hum of engines coming up from the south. I tried to judge their progress by the steadily increasing volume of sound, a mental chore that was interrupted by a sudden roaring explosion. Sixteen bombs had been released by mistake from the American planes; several of them hit near my command post, sending fragments flying all over the place, but fortunately injuring no one, except the feelings of my police dog, Mike, who at that time was the proud mother of six week-old pups. (*Clark, 1954*)

After the war, Clark sought to vindicate his part in the decision to bomb the monastery:

> Not only was the bombing of the Abbey an unnecessary psychological mistake in the propaganda field, but it was a tactical military mistake of the first magnitude. It only made our job more difficult, more costly in terms of men, machines and time. (*Clark, 1954*)

When Alexander was asked after the war if the destruction of the monastery was a military necessity and whether it was morally wrong, he answered:

> The answer to the first question is 'yes'. It was necessary more for the effect it would have on the morale of the attackers than for purely material reasons. The answer to the second question is this: when soldiers are fighting for a just cause and are prepared to suffer death and mutilation in the process, bricks and mortar, no matter how venerable, cannot be allowed to weigh against human lives. (*North, 1962*)

Kesselring sought to gain the maximum propaganda value from the destruction, telling Radio Berlin:

> I have only the deepest contempt for the cynical mendacity and sanctimonious pictures with which the Anglo-Saxon Commands now attempt to make me responsible for their acts. (*Collier, 1983*)

Radio Berlin also reported that when Cardinal Maglione was told that the Americans intended to rebuild the monastery after the war, the

Cardinal replied: 'Even if you rebuild it in gold and diamonds, it still isn't the monastery.' (*Collier, 1983*)

On the afternoon of 11 February and through the next day, an aggressive follow-up bombardment of artillery and a raid by fifty-nine fighter bombers rained down on the monastery. However, the air raid had not been coordinated with ground commands, and an immediate infantry follow-up failed to materialise. Its timing had been driven by the United States Air Force, which viewed the bombing as a separate operation. They took more account of the clear weather than the needs of the ground forces, who were neither consulted nor informed of the timing of the aerial assault.

The brigade commanders of the Indian troops were having a morning planning meeting when they heard the American bombers flying over their heads. Many of their troops had only taken up their positions two days previously, and there had been difficulties in supplying them with sufficient supplies for a full-scale assault because of constant wet weather and flooding. They certainly were not ready for mounting an assault on Cassino.

Following its destruction, and with its sacredness violated, German paratroopers then occupied the ruins of the abbey and turned it into a fortress. On the night following the bombing, British troops attacked from their position just 64m away on Snakeshead Ridge. The assault failed, with heavy losses.

What the Allied commanders had not considered was that while the monastery remained intact it was unsatisfactory as a defensive position. After it had been destroyed it was left as a jagged heap of broken masonry and debris, which was perfect for hiding heavy guns and mortars.

The following night British troops were ordered to attack again, but without artillery support. This was because of the risk of killing Allied troops on the slopes with friendly fire. The attack went in at midnight, but the German defence held firm, and the troops were beaten off, once again with many losses. Over the two nights, the Royal Sussex Regiment lost twelve out of fifteen officers and 162 out of 313 men in this futile waste of human life.

Pope Pius remained diplomatically silent in public about the destruction of the monastery, but his Cardinal Secretary of State, Luigi Maglione, told the senior American diplomat to the Vatican that the bombing was 'a colossal blunder ... a piece of a gross stupidity'. (*Richardson, 1984*)

All the evidence available to this day suggests that there were no German troops in the monastery and that the only people killed were

230 Italian civilians who had taken refuge there believing it to be safe. They were part of a larger group of refugees including the abbot and six monks, three tenant farmer families, and orphaned or abandoned children who had survived in the deep vaults of the abbey.

At 7.30 a.m. on 17 February, the old abbot led the group down the mule path towards the Liri valley, reciting the rosary. After they arrived at a German first-aid station, some of the seriously wounded were taken away in a German military ambulance and the monks were taken to the monastery of Sant'Anselmo all'Aventino by German troops.

That night, yet another assault was launched on Cassino. The attack along Snakeshead Ridge was led by Indian troops, with the depleted Royal Sussex Regiment held in reserve. Gurkha Rifles were ordered to attack at a different point of the mountain, while other Gurkhas were to cross the difficult terrain on slopes and ravines in a direct assault on the monastery. The hope of the Allied commanders was that the Gurkhas' mountain warfare skills would enable them to succeed where others had failed. This proved a faint hope. Once again, the fighting was brutal, but no progress was made, and casualties were heavy. After the Indians lost 196 officers and men and the Gurkhas had lost 244, the attack was called off on the following day. Yet another futile waste of human life for nothing.

In the other half of the main assault, the two New Zealand Māori companies[47] forced a crossing of the Liri and attempted to capture the railway station in Cassino town. The intention was to allow engineers to build a causeway that could be used by armoured support. With the aid of a nearly constant smokescreen laid down by Allied artillery, the Māori were able to hold their positions for much of the day. However, their isolation and lack of both armoured supports made their situation hopeless. When it became clear that the hoped-for breakthrough had not been achieved, they were ordered to pull back to the river. Ironically, the battle for Cassino railway station had been remarkably close. The Germans had not expected their counterattack to succeed. They had been incredibly lucky indeed.

47 Despite some opposition from elders, several thousand Māori served with the Allied forces during the Second World War. As one of the volunteers later wrote: 'Their request could not be denied them by their elders and chieftains, all their long history had been steeped in the religion of war, and the training of the Maori child from his infancy to manhood was aimed at the perfection of the warrior-class, while to die in the pursuit of the War God Tumatauenga was a sacred duty and a manly death.'

For the third assault, it was decided that crossing the Gari river downstream of Cassino town was an unattractive option while the winter weather persisted. It was decided therefore to launch twin attacks from the north along the Liri valley: one towards Cassino town and the other towards the monastery.

The British troops who had arrived in late February 1944 and been placed under the command of the New Zealand Corps would then cross the Liri downstream of Cassino and start the push to Rome. Freyberg ordered a bombing and shelling of the town of Cassino, which had already been ruined and deserted, in order that the New Zealand and British troops would be left with just a 'mopping up operation'. (*Merlin, 2008*)

The bombing plan was for nearly 500 aircraft (ten groups of heavy bombers and six groups of medium bombers) to attack the town in relays. Immediately following the bombing, at 12 p.m. troops were to advance, behind a creeping barrage of artillery fire aimed at the German defences in the town. Tanks would be deployed from the north at 2 p.m. The troops would then continue south through the town to the railway. While all this was going on, Indian troops would be working step by step along the eastern slopes of Monte Cassino, while other Indian troops would be maintaining pressure on the defenders in the ruins of the monastery.

None of the other Allied commanders were happy with the plan, but it was hoped that the massive bombing of Cassino town would prove to be the trump card. To avoid taking vehicles across waterlogged ground, three clear days of good weather were required, and for twenty-one successive days the assault had to be postponed as the troops waited in the freezing wet positions for a better weather forecast. Morale was not helped when, on 2 March, the New Zealand General Howard Kippenberger was seriously wounded on the slopes of Mount Trocchio. He had climbed Trocchio to gain a better view of the Cassino battlefield. Near the top of the mountain, he triggered a land mine, which exploded and injured both his legs. One of his feet was severed in the blast. He was evacuated to the FSU, where his other foot and the lower portions of both legs were amputated.

Then Vesuvius began to rumble, and tremors were felt in the surrounding countryside as small flakes of red-hot ash rained down, burning holes in shirts and uniforms. At the local observatory, the senior volcanologist, Professor Imbo, warned the military authorities at Caserta of the imminent danger to the Naples area and that the RAF fighter station at Terzigno would probably be in the path of the lava flow.

On 13 March, after much rumbling underfoot, the skies filled with ash as torrents of lava burst forth and for the next few days the troops massing for the assault on Cassino had a front-row seat at one of the nature's wonders. The stream of molten lava was visible for miles and lit up the night sky. After two days the molten lava split into two flows like an inverted 'Y' and was set to engulf the twin hamlets of San Sebastiano and Vesuvio a Massa.

The 67th FSU was approached for help with the aged and infirm. Although they could not allow the use of ambulances because of the impending battle, volunteers were called for to go with an Austin K2/Y truck to assist with the removal of people and their goods. As the trucks arrived in San Sebastiano, there was a large, red glowing fire from the lava stream from the volcano.

The heat was blistering, and every so often large burning pieces of red molten rock would fall ever closer. Finally, the truck was loaded. There was no panic and the poor people were just grateful for the little that the British troops could do for them.

Once the lava ceased to flow at night and the streams that had submerged the two little hamlets began to cool and set hard, a huge black smoke pillar billowed thousands of feet from the centre of the crater. Luckily there was no immediate wind, but after four days a strong breeze carried a huge smokescreen seawards towards the Isle of Capri and Ischia.

The third battle of Cassino commenced at 8.30 a.m. on 15 March with a bombardment of 750 tonnes of heavy bombs with delayed-action fuses. The barrage lasted three and a half hours, but unfortunately only half of the bombs landed within 2km of the target and only one in twelve fell within 1,000m.

Following a creeping barrage put up by 746 heavy guns, the New Zealanders set off on their advance and killed about half the 300 German paratroopers in the town. However, the German defences rallied quickly, and the advance of the Allied heavy guns and tanks was held up by bomb craters. By the time a follow-up assault had been ordered, it was too late. German defences had been reorganised, and the rain had started. Small lakes formed in the bomb craters, and the rain interfered with the operation of Allied radio sets. The dark clouds also blotted out the moonlight, hindering the task of clearing routes through the potholes.

On the right, the New Zealanders captured Rocca Janula (often referred to as Castle Hill), the tenth-century castle that dominates Cassino town, but the Indian Infantry were repelled. In the confusion of the fight, a company of Gurkhas took a track that managed to capture a German defensive position further up the hill. By the end of 17 March, the Gurkhas were just 230m from the monastery, but their lines of supply were compromised by the German positions.

Although the town of Cassino was still fiercely defended, New Zealand units managed to capture Cassino Station, but the Germans were able to bring in reinforcements and they managed to place snipers back into parts of the town that had supposedly been cleared.

The Allied commanders decided that 19 March was the date for the decisive assault on Cassino town and on the monastery, including a surprise attack by tanks working their way along an old logging road (referred to as 'Cavendish Road') from Caira to Albaneta Farm. This road had been made ready for the tanks and heavy armour by units of engineers working under cover of darkness. However, a surprise counterattack by German paratroopers completely disrupted any possibility of an assault that day. Without infantry support the Allied tanks were all knocked out by mid-afternoon. In the town, the attackers made little progress, and the initiative returned to the Germans.

On 20 March, Freyberg committed additional troops to the battle, firstly to provide an increased presence in the town so that cleared areas would not be reinfiltrated by the Germans, and secondly to allow men to be released from the slopes of Cassino to close off the two routes that were being used by the Germans to bring in reinforcements. As the fighting continued the Allied commanders felt they were on the brink of success, but the Germans stood firm, and the attack failed. Progress was painfully slow as the troops were forced to fight from house to house.

By this time, Churchill was becoming increasingly frustrated by the slow progress and ever ready to try to dictate strategy. He wrote to Alexander:

> I wish you would explain to me why this passage to Cassino, Monastery Hill etc all on a front of two or three miles is the only place which you must keep butting at. About five or six divisions have been worn out going into those jaws. (*Wallace, 1987*)

On 23 March Alexander met with his commanders and a range of views were expressed, but it was evident to all that the New Zealand and Indian troops were exhausted. Freyberg decided that the attack could not continue. The German paratroopers had held their ground.

The next three days were spent extracting the isolated Gurkhas and New Zealand troops from the slopes. The Allied line was reorganised and reinforced by British troops. In their time on the Cassino front line, the Indians had lost 3,000 killed, missing, or wounded and the New Zealanders had lost 1,600 men.

Meanwhile in Rome, a column of German troops were singing as they marched through the Piazza di Spagna into the narrow street of Via Rasella. The troops were ethnic German speakers from the north Italian province of South Tyrol. The march was intended to intimidate and suppress the Italian Resistance.

The troops were ambushed by twelve communist partisans using an improvised explosive device consisting of 12kg of TNT packed in a steel case. This was inserted into a bag containing an additional 6kg of TNT and TNT-filled iron tubing. The device, which had been pushed into position by a partisan disguised as a street cleaner, caused the immediate deaths of twenty-eight German troops and two civilian bystanders,

In retaliation, German and Italian troops rounded up Roman civilians in front of the Palazzo Barberini, and the order was given to execute ten Italians for each of the German troops who were killed, stipulating that the executions should be carried out within twenty-four hours.

Because of the time limit that had been imposed, it was decided that the victims would have to be shot in the back of the head at close range rather than by conventional firing squad. The massacre was carried out in a rural suburb of the city, inside the tunnels of the disused quarries of Pozzolana, near the Via Ardeatina.

A total of 335 Italian prisoners were taken, more than the order called for. Because the execution squad consisted of several officers who had never killed anyone before, several cases of cognac were delivered to the caves to calm the officers' nerves. The officers were ordered to lead the prisoners into the caves with their hands tied behind their backs and then have them kneel so that no more than one bullet would be needed for each prisoner. Many were forced to kneel over the bodies of those who had been killed before them because the cave had become filled with dead bodies. During the killings, the existence of the extra prisoners was discovered, and it was decided to kill them anyway, to prevent the place of execution from becoming known.

I did not learn about this massacre until I was back home at Mount Vernon Hospital, but if I ever had doubts about what I had been fighting for and whether my sacrifice was justified, those doubts disappeared that day. However, later I began to wonder. Was this massacre really any worse than that perpetrated by American GIs at Santo Pietro? War makes barbarians of us all.

The Fourth Battle of Monte Cassino (code-named *Operation Diadem*) aimed to break the German defences on the Gustav Line and open the Liri Valley for an advance on Rome. *Diadem* was designed to coincide with the invasion of Normandy, so the German forces that would be tied down in Italy could not be redeployed to France. Churchill and Roosevelt also hoped that the liberation of Rome would boost the morale of the thousands of troops who were preparing for the cross-Channel invasion.

The 8th Army was a mixture of Polish, Indian, Canadian and British troops. The 5th Army contingent consisted of French (including Moroccan Goumiers) and American troops.

Diadem was launched at 2300 on 11 May 1944 by elements of the British and Indian infantry, with supporting fire from the Canadians. Despite fierce German opposition, they made a successful night crossing of the Gari and Liri rivers, breaking through the German defences.

The first Polish objective was Monte Calvario, just north of Monte Cassino. The next three days saw the Polish infantry involved in bitter fighting against the German paratroopers, and both sides suffered heavy losses in the mud and rain. The leading Polish battalions had been nearly wiped out, suffering 4,000 casualties, and by 15 May the attack had to be called off. Mount Calvary was referred to as a 'miniature Verdun'. (*Hamilton, 2011*)

Further south, it was the French-led Algerians and Moroccans who had achieved the decisive penetration. The Germans were terrified of the knife-wielding North Africans, who demonstrated alarming aggressiveness and favoured night attacks. As British reinforcements came up to help the Poles and complete the encirclement, the Polish troops prepared for another attempt on Monte Cassino. Under constant artillery and mortar fire, the infantry clawed its way up the slopes. Fighting was hand-to-hand, but the Poles struggled past the German paratroopers and began to push them back. By nightfall, the situation was uncertain, but by 18 May the Polish flag flew over Monte Cassino. The attacking forces had been so battered and were so weary that it had taken time to find a man with even the strength to raise the flag. As Mark Clark commented later: 'The Polish Corps fought with utter bravery and disregard for casualties.' (*Clark, 1954*)

The importance of Cassino has continued to be debated by historians. The American government's official position changed over a quarter of a century. The assertion that the German use of the monastery was 'irrefutable' was removed from the record in 1961 by the Office of the Chief of Military History. A congressional inquiry that reported to House of Representatives in the twentieth anniversary year of the bombing stated: 'It appears that no German troops, except a small military police detachment, were actually inside the abbey before the bombing.' (*Rennie, 2021*)

The final change to the American Army's official record was made in 1969 and concluded that 'the abbey was actually unoccupied by German troops'. (*Office of the Chief of Military History, U.S. Army, 1969*)

Although Eisenhower and Alexander were right that lives were more important than buildings, if the strategy was to save lives, it failed miserably and disgracefully. The Allies suffered around 55,000 casualties in the campaign. German casualty figures are estimated at around 20,000 killed and wounded. Could anything really justify the wanton destruction of human life on this scale? It was no problem for Churchill. He barely mentioned the losses at Cassino, preferring to focus on the fact that the battle detained German troops who might otherwise have been defending occupied France.

Following the capture of Cassino, the way was now clear for the Allies to move on Rome. On 23 May, Allied troops attacked the Hitler Line that ran through Piedmonte, Pontecorvo, and Aquino in central Italy, while at the same time American troops were finally able to move out of the Anzio beachhead. The Hitler Line was breached by the Canadian troops at Pontecorvo on 23 May and the Germans were forced to retreat further to the north-west.

Despite Alexander's overall plan for *Diadem* requiring American troops to strike inland and cut Route 6, Clark asked Truscott to prepare alternatives and to be ready to switch from one to another at forty-eight hours' notice. Of the four scenarios prepared by Truscott, *Operation Buffalo* called for an attack through Cisterna, into the gap in the hills and to cut Route 6 at Valmontone. *Operation Turtle,* on the other hand, foresaw a main thrust to the left of the Alban Hills, taking Campoleone, Albano and on to Rome. On 5 May, Alexander selected Operation Buffalo and issued Clark with orders to this effect. However, Clark was determined that his troops should get to Rome before anyone else, as evidenced in his later writing:

> We not only wanted the honour of capturing Rome, but felt that we deserved it ... Not only did we intend to become the first army to seize Rome from the south, but we intended to see that people at home knew that it was the 5th Army that did the job, and knew the price that had been paid for it. (*Clark L, 2006*)

On the evening of 25 May, Truscott received new orders from Clark to implement *Operation Turtle* and turn the main line of attack 90 degrees to the left. Clark informed Alexander of these developments late in the morning of 26 May, by which time the change of orders was a fait accompli.

There is much dispute about his rationale. It has been suggested that Clark was so obsessed with the notion that the British 8th Army, who were advancing up the Liri Valley, might get there before him that he issued an order that any British soldier seen in Rome before the US 5th Army would be shot.

So where did this accusation originate from? It has been suggested by the historian James Holland (in his book *Italy's Sorrow: A Year of War, 1944–1945*) that the story originated from Raleigh Trevelyan, the British author, who served with the Green Howards battalion at Anzio. In Trevelyan's account, written in 1960, he cited Harold Macmillan, claiming Alexander was 'furious' when he discovered Clark had 'disobeyed' his orders over Valmontone. However, there is no mention of this in Macmillan's diaries. Furthermore, Alexander had clearly laid down before the battle that Rome was allocated to the 5th Army, while the 8th Army was constantly reminded that their job was to bypass Rome and continue northwards.

Wherever it came from, the story spread like wildfire after the war. There is one authentic source to back up Trevelyan's allegations and that was Truscott himself. He wrote later:

> … I was dumbfounded. This was no time to drive to the north-west where the enemy was still strong; we should pour our maximum power into the Valmontone Gap to ensure the destruction of the retreating German Army. I would not comply with the order without first talking to General Clark in person. … [However], he was not on the beachhead and could not be reached even by radio … such was the order that turned the main effort of the beachhead forces from the Valmontone Gap and prevented destruction of the German 10th Army. (*Majdalany, 1957*)

He went on to write:

> There has never been any doubt in my mind that had General Clark held loyally to General Alexander's instructions, had he not changed the direction of my attack to the north-west on May 26, the strategic objectives of Anzio would have been accomplished in full. To be first in Rome was a poor compensation for this lost opportunity. (*Majdalany, 1957*)

Clark's change of plan resulted in 44,000 casualties and failed in its objective of destroying the German 10th Army. It also condemned the Allies to another year of fighting in Italy.

For all that, neither Alexander nor Churchill took issue with Clark, apparently accepting that the prize was worth the sacrifice. It is indeed beyond dispute that the city of Rome was of great strategic importance, not only because of its airfields and extensive road and rail networks, but also because of its status as a great and ancient city of culture. Rome had been under German occupation for nine months since September 1943, but after Hitler decided that it should not be defended, it had been declared an open city. This signalled to the Allies that the minimum force would be necessary to take control of the city. Conditions in Rome were not as bad as in some parts of Europe. The city's water supply was unaffected and there was working electricity. However, food supplies were now running low, and Clark knew that the arrival of Allied troops would be welcomed by the Roman people. As a prize it was simply too tempting for Clark, whose desire was to be seen as a conquering hero, no matter the human cost.

On 5 June 1944, the people of Rome flooded into the streets to welcome the arrival of the American troops. Shops and workplaces were closed for the day and Pope Pius XII appeared on the balcony of the Vatican to address the crowds below in St Peter's Square. He gave thanks for this victory and praised the 'goodwill on both sides', since the city had survived its occupation and liberation largely intact.

The British and American military authorities, in a broadcast from London shortly after the event, were in an equally celebratory mood, describing the campaign as 'daring, unconventional and brilliant'. Churchill himself told Parliament:

> Today we have had the joyful tidings that the Allied forces have made a successful entry into Rome, and it is indeed a memorable and glorious event in the annals of the war. The capture of Rome is a clear indication that the enemy has been driven out, and this represents a significant milestone in our campaign. It rewards the intense fighting of the last five months. (*HMSO, 1944*)

The Roman people hoped that the capture of Rome would resolve the political crisis that followed the removal of Mussolini and that the resources of the Allies would solve the shortage of food. The reality was that the Americans did not regard the Italians as allies, but as a defeated enemy who had killed many of their comrades. Italy could not be welcomed back into the company of nations until it had rejected both fascism and communism.

To Clark, the capture of Rome was his defining personal achievement. At the train station of Centocelle on the Via Casilina there was a large illuminated 'Roma' sign. Clark had several photographs taken of him standing under the sign and these appeared in the press around the world.

However, Clark's bravado did not impress everyone. Captain Giles Lampson, the son of the British ambassador in Cairo, and Clark's British aide de camp, found Clark's attitude hard to accept. He wrote to his fiancée: 'One thing does rile me a lot here, and that is the enormous amount of personal publicity and boasting that goes on. One cannot move without fifteen press photographers in tow.' All the generals received fan mail and kept albums of photographs and scrapbooks of press cuttings as though it was the most normal thing in the world. 'However,' added Giles, 'if that is the way the American public wants its news and if it is going to stimulate interest in the war and help recruiting and so forth, then they are right to do it. But it strikes me as rather indecent and ostentatious.' (*Holland, Italy's Sorrow, 2008*)

Others were more critical. Clark's failure to follow orders and the perceived waste of lives as a result led British war correspondent Alan Whicker to observe: 'If he had been German, Hitler would have had him shot.' (*Whicker, 2006*)

In May 1945, on Memorial Day, Truscott returned to the Rome-Sicily cemetery at Nettuno, (near Anzio), where thousands of American troops were buried. According to Second World War cartoonist Bill Mauldin, Truscott turned his back on the dignitaries assembled there and started to address the graves of the fallen servicemen buried there, saying:

> ... everyone tells leaders it is not their fault that men get killed in war, but every leader knows in his heart that is not altogether true. If any of my men are present here through a mistake of mine, I ask that they would forgive me, but I recognise that this is asking a hell of a lot under the circumstances. I won't stand to listen to older men speak that death on the battlefield was glorious. I don't see much glory in getting killed in your late teens or early 20s. If I ever encounter such living men, I will straighten them out on behalf of you. (*Este, 2017*)

The propaganda value of the Allied occupation of Rome was offset by the reality that Kesselring's forces were able to retreat not in a rout but in an orderly fashion. Seven divisions made it to the next line of defence, where they were able to link up with other German troops and then make a fighting withdrawal to the Gothic Line north of Florence.

Florence, 250km north of Rome, did not fall to the Allies until 13 August and by that time the Germans had made ready yet another chain of defences – the Gothic Line – running from the Tyrrhenian coast midway between Pisa and La Spezia, over the Apennines in a reversed 'S' curve, to the Adriatic coast between Pesaro and Rimini.

Alexander might have made more headway against Kesselring's new front if some of his forces had not been needed elsewhere, but the Italian Front came to be seen as being of secondary importance to the offensives through France. This was underlined by the withdrawal of seven divisions from the 5th Army during the summer of 1944 for the American-sponsored but eventually unnecessary invasion of southern France (code-named *Operation Anvil*). By 5 August, the strength of the 5th Army had fallen from 249,000 to 153,000, and they had only eighteen divisions to confront the combined German strength of fourteen divisions plus between four and seven reserve divisions.

The British 8th Army, switched back from the west to the Adriatic coast, and achieved only an indecisive breakthrough toward Rimini before the autumn rains set in, which made it even more difficult against Kesselring's resolute opposition.

Hitler was worried about the state of preparation of the Gothic Line and feared that the Allies would use amphibious landings to outflank its defences. Using more than 15,000 slave labourers, the Germans created more than 2,000 fortified machine gun nests, casemates, bunkers, observation posts and artillery fighting positions.

Alexander's original plan was to storm the Gothic Line in the centre, where most of his forces were already concentrated. It was the shortest route to the plains of Lombardy, and the assault could be mounted quickly. He also proposed a deception operation to convince the Germans that the main blow would come on the Adriatic.

On 4 August, Alexander met the commander of the 8th Army, Lieutenant General Oliver Leese, but found that he did not support the plan. He argued that the Allies had lost their specialist French mountain troops to the invasion of southern France and that the 8th Army's strength, which lay in combining infantry, armour and guns, could not be employed in the high mountains of the central Apennines.

Operation Olive, as the new offensive was badged, called for Leese's 8th Army to attack up the Adriatic coast toward Pesaro and Rimini and draw in the German reserves from the centre of the country. Clark's 5th Army would then attack in the weakened central Apennines north of Florence toward Bologna with British troops on the right wing of the attack fanning toward the coast to create a pincer with the 8th Army advance. This meant that the 8th Army had to be moved from the centre of Italy to the Adriatic coast. This took two weeks, while a new intelligence deception plan (*Operation Ulster*) was undertaken to convince Kesselring that the main attack would be in central Italy.

On 25 August the British 8th Army crossed the Metauro river and launched its attack against the Gothic Line, while Polish and Canadian troops on the coast advanced towards Pesaro. The Germans were taken by surprise, to the extent that two of the key commanders were away on leave as the assault began. Kesselring himself was uncertain whether this was the start of a major offensive or just the 8th Army advancing to occupy vacated ground while the main Allied attack would come on the 5th Army front towards Bologna. On 27 August, he was still expressing the view that the attack was a diversion but on the following day he was supplied with a copy of Leese's orders. Kesselring then realised that a major offensive was under way. In response, he ordered three divisions of reinforcements from Bologna to the Adriatic front, but it took more than two days to get them into position.

By 30 August, the Canadian and British Corps had reached the main German defensive positions running along the Foglia river. Taking advantage of the Germans' lack of manpower, the Canadians penetrated the defences and by 3 September they had advanced a further 24km to the defences running from the coast near Riccione. The Allies were close to breaking through to Rimini, but fierce resistance from German paratroopers and intense artillery fire brought the advance to a halt.

Meanwhile, British troops were finding progress equally tough in the more difficult hill country with its poor roads. On 3 September, while the Canadians once again attacked along the coastal plain, the British made an armoured attack to reach the Marano river. The aim here was to open the way to the plains beyond, which could be rapidly exploited by British tanks. However, after two days of fighting with heavy losses on both sides, the Allies called off their assault to rethink their strategy.

After eleven assaults between 4 and 13 September by British troops, Indian troops made a successful attack on 15 September. To the north, a similarly bloody engagement was being fought out at Croce. The Germans held their positions, and it took five days of fighting before the British troops captured the town.

The way was open to Rimini as Kesselring's forces had taken heavy losses, and three divisions of reinforcements ordered to the Adriatic front would not be available for at least a day. However, once again, torrential rain turned the rivers into torrents and stopped air operations. As the Allied assault ground to a crawl, the German defenders had the opportunity to reorganise and reinforce their positions on the Marano river. Once more, the 8th Army was confronted by an organised line of defence: the Rimini Line.

Churchill urged Alexander to break through the German defences to open up the route through the 'Ljubljana Gap' into Austria and Hungary. While this would threaten Germany, Churchill's primary concern was to forestall the Russians, who were now advancing into central Europe. Initially, the American Chiefs of Staff had strongly opposed this strategy but following the Allied successes in France during the summer they relented.

Meanwhile, with Croce and Montescudo secured, the 8th Army advanced to the Marano river and the frontier of the principality of San Marino. By 19 September, San Marino was isolated and fell to the Allies. Only 4.8km beyond San Marino lay the Marecchia valley running across the 8th Army line of advance and down to the sea at Rimini. During the night of 19 September, the German anti-tank gunners had a field day. Twenty-four Allied tanks were destroyed, and sixty-four tank crew were killed. Just three Sherman tanks survived the onslaught.

Canadian troops broke the German positions on the Ausa river on 20 September and Greek troops entered Rimini on the morning of 21 September as the Germans withdrew to new positions on the Marecchia. However, Kesselring's strong defences had won him time until the autumn rains came. Progress for the 8th Army became slow, with mud and water making it difficult to keep roads and tracks open. The 8th Army found themselves confronted, once again, by a succession of swollen rivers running across their line of advance and preventing their tanks and armour from exploiting the breakthrough. The British, Canadian and New Zealand infantry had to grind their way forward while the Germans withdrew their forces behind the Uso river, a few miles beyond Rimini.

The German positions on the Uso were finally overcome on 26 September, and the 8th Army reached the next river, the Fiumicino, the following day. Four days of heavy rain forced a halt, and by this time the Allied troops were exhausted. Since the start of *Operation Olive*, the 8th Army had suffered 14,000 casualties and the Germans 16,000.

Clark's plan was for American troops to strike along the road from Florence to Firenzuola and Imola to outflank the German defences on the main Florence to Bologna Road, while on their right British troops would advance through the Gothic Line to cut Kesselring's communications at Faenza.

The fighting toward Imola had drawn German troops from Bologna, and Clark decided to switch his main thrust back towards Bologna. American troops pushed steadily onward and by 2 October they had reached Monghidoro, some 32km from Bologna. However, yet again, rain and low cloud prevented air support while the roads back to the supply dumps near Florence had become impassable.

On 5 October, American troops renewed their offensive along a 23km front to Bologna. They were supported on their right flank by British troops, newly returned to Italy after a three-month recuperation in Egypt. The weather cleared on the morning of 10 October to allow artillery and air support to be brought in. By the second half of October, it was becoming increasingly clear to Alexander that with the winter coming on and exhaustion and combat losses increasingly affecting his forces' capabilities, no breakthrough was going to happen any time soon.

On the Adriatic front, the British 8th Army's advance resumed through the Apennine foothills toward Forlì. Indian troops crossed the Fiumicino river high in the hills and turned the German defensive line on the river, forcing the German troops downstream towards Bologna. Paradoxically, this helped Kesselring because it shortened the front he had to defend and the distance between his two armies, providing him with greater flexibility to switch units between the two fronts.

Continuing their push, the British troops crossed the Savio river, which runs north-eastward to the Adriatic, and by 25 October they were closing on the Ronco river, some 16km beyond the Savio, behind which the Germans had withdrawn. By the end of the month, the advance had reached Forlì, halfway between Rimini and Bologna.

Cutting German communications remained a key objective. Indeed, later Kesselring was to say that if the front south of Bologna could not be held, then all the German positions east of Bologna 'were automatically gone'. Alexander and Clark decided to make a last push for Bologna before winter set in.

The Allies in Italy were short of artillery ammunition because of the focus on the final assault on Germany. Nevertheless, American and British artillery pounded away for the next eleven days. Little progress was made in the centre along the main road to Bologna, but on the right, things were going better and on 20 October American troops seized Monte Grande. Three days later British troops stormed Monte Spaduro, but the remaining 6.4km were over difficult terrain, and the German troops were reinforced by three of the best German divisions, which Kesselring had been able to withdraw from the Romagna.

By late October, Brazilian[48] troops had pushed the German forces through the province of Lucca to Barga, where their advance was

48 Brazil's involvement in the Italian campaign of 1944 was unusual but historically significant. It was the only South American country to send troops to fight in Europe during World War II. At the start of WWII Brazil remained neutral, but after several Brazilian merchant ships were sunk with heavy civilian loss of life, Brazil declared war on Germany and Italy. The Brazilian Expeditionary Force (FEB) that served in Italy consisted of about 25,000 troops who were assigned to the U.S. Fifth Army.

halted. In early November, the build-up of Brazilian troops and some American reinforcements had not compensated the 5th Army for the troops diverted to France. The situation in the British 8th Army was even worse: replacement British and Canadian troops were also being diverted to northern Europe. The problem now was that the Allies had too much armour and too few men.

During November and December, the 5th Army concentrated on dislodging the Germans from their well-placed artillery positions, which had been key in preventing the Allied advance towards Bologna and the Po Valley. However, the German defences around Monte Castello proved extremely resilient.

Meanwhile, the British 8th Army commenced a drive up the Adriatic coast and captured Ravenna on 5 November, crossing the Montone river on 9 November. However, the going continued to be very tough and it was not until 23 November that they crossed the Cosina river.

By 17 December, the Lamone river had been crossed and the German Army then established itself on its raised banks, high above the surrounding plain that ran across the line of the 8th Army advance. With snows falling and winter firmly set in, any attempt to cross the Senio was out of the question and so the 8th Army's 1944 campaign ended.

In late December, in a final flourish, the Germans used a predominantly Italian force of units to attack the 5th Army in the Serchio valley to pin Allied units there that might otherwise have been switched to the central front. Two brigades of Indian Infantry were rapidly switched across the Apennines to reinforce the Americans but by the time they had arrived the German forces had broken through to capture Barga and this was not regained until the New Year.

In mid-December, Harold Alexander was made supreme commander of the Mediterranean Theatre and Mark Clark took his place as commander of the Allied Armies in Italy. Command of the US 5th Army then passed to Lucian Truscott.

When the winter weather improved by mid-February, the 5th Army resumed its attacks on German artillery positions in Operation Encore. By 5 March, the way through the northern Apennines to the Po valley was clear and Kesselring began to prepare for the final withdrawal of German troops from Italy. After nearly twenty months of fighting in the 'soft underbelly', the end of the war was in sight.

Chapter 19

AFTERMATH

When I think back on the Second World War I am doubly conflicted. There is no doubt in my mind that Hitler was evil and needed to be defeated, but I never hated the German people and never understood why I was supposed to want to kill them. I saw German soldiers – dead and alive – in Italy and I thought how similar they looked to my comrades. What had they ever done to me? I saw plenty of American troops too and realised that they were just like us, and just as scared.

Churchill claimed that the Italian campaign was worth it because it inflicted half a million German casualties and drew forces away from France, but was that really what it was all about? The original purpose was not to fight a war of attrition, but to bring a quick end to the conflict. In that regard it was a failure. Italy never was a 'soft underbelly' or an easy route to Germany.

The Italian campaign was not a glamorous chapter in the war and few films were made about the traumatising slog from mountain to mountain. After the war, the American survivors of the campaign lobbied for a Congressional hearing to seek redress for the many mistakes made by the Allied commanders. During two days of hearings, the thirty committee members heard testimony from veterans including Lucien Truscott, who referred to the first assault on Cassino and the battle of Garigliano as: 'the most colossal blunders of the Second World War and a murderous blunder and that every man connected with this undertaking knew ... was doomed to failure before it took place'. (*Merlin, 2008*)

The resolutions charged Mark Clark with a clear disregard for human life and military information. Clark, they alleged, ordered the attack even though he knew it was going to fail with horrendous losses, even after his subordinates had voiced their misgivings and offered alternative suggestions for attacks elsewhere that could, and later did, succeed.

The petitioners urged Congress to investigate not just the 'Garigliano river fiasco', but to 'Take the necessary steps to correct a military system that will permit an inefficient and inexperienced officer, such as Gen. Mark Clark, in a high command ... to prevent future soldiers from being sacrificed wastefully and uselessly'. (*The Pictorial History of the 36th Infantry 'Texas' Division*, 1946)

However, to no one's great surprise, although the hearing criticised Clark for his decision to proceed with the assault despite unfavourable conditions and made recommendations to reform military leadership and decision-making processes to avoid similar tragedies in the future, it did not prevent Clark from being given command of the United Nations forces and the US Army forces in the Far East during the Korean War. Around 70,000 Allied soldiers died in the Italian campaign because of poor decision-making, but once again, no one was at fault. No one was to blame.

Chapter 20

REHABILITATION

I now need to take you back to January 1944 when I was repatriated to the UK on the *Llandovery Castle*. On landing at Tilbury Docks, I was taken to Mount Vernon Hospital at Northwood. At the height of the war, the hospital had more than 1,000 beds for injured British and French servicemen, as well as some German prisoners of war. I was put in a ward in a hut that had been built before the war to accommodate the anticipated casualties.

I felt bitter and angry; my life had been ruined but for what purpose? I did not hate the Germans or the Italians, but I detested the British establishment and military hierarchy that required so many sacrifices of the ordinary man but made very few themselves.

At Mount Vernon, I was slowly nursed back to health and I read extensively and voraciously about the background to the war, the Italian campaign, and American and Irish history. After several weeks, I was given a pair of crutches to help me move around. The surgeons decided to leave the shrapnel in my arm. It never troubled me greatly, even though it was still highly visible under my skin.

As I was still a serving soldier, I was confined to the hospital, but as soon as I was well enough, I left and returned to my parents' flat in Drury Lane. Only a few days after arriving back in London I was woken by a party of red caps who had come to arrest me as an absconder. Pointing to my empty trouser leg, I asked: 'Have I not done my bit?' With embarrassed apologies they turned and left.

The flat at Drury Lane was up several flights of stairs, but I became expert at placing the crutches six or seven steps ahead of me and then swinging my body to the landing below. I needed to do this quite often as the V1 flying bombs[49] began to fall on London as we all rushed to the underground shelter in Betterton Street. I prided myself in being able to get up and down the stairs faster than an able-bodied person. This skill came in extremely helpful one night in 1944 when I heard the ominous phut-phut of a V1 flying very low overhead.

When the noise stopped, I launched myself down the flights of stairs to emerge into Drury Lane just as the bomb exploded on the Daily Herald offices at the Odhams Press in Long Acre. Although shaken by the explosion, I was otherwise uninjured. The falling flying bomb and the resulting explosion were captured by a Daily Mirror photographer and published in the paper several months after the event so as not to spread alarm.

I was finally discharged from the Army on 15 August 1945 just a few weeks after the 1945 General Election. I was paid £41 (or 10 shillings per month for thirty-one months) to cover my service to 9 September 1945. I also received a set of civilian clothing, which included a suit, a shirt, underclothes, a raincoat, hat, and shoes.

I have always been amazed that people were surprised at the outcome of the 1945 General Election. Churchill didn't just lose it, he was rejected totally by the British people. The fact is, Labour had an ambitious programme of change while Churchill offered nothing but a return to the old ways of privilege and social inequality. After six years of war, we were all fed up and wanted a fresh start.

Churchill took the 1945 defeat badly and lapsed into depression. He turned his attention to ensuring that his version of the events of the war would be the one that would be remembered. Working with a team of researchers, he was given unparallelled access that enabled him to 'curate' the official papers, pulling together minutes and telegrams to ensure that his role in the war was presented as he wanted it to be remembered. The result was the six-volume series, *The Second World War*.

Churchill largely succeeded in his aims and his version is the one that prevails in folk memory. Churchill's faults and failings are largely excused and forgiven. For my part, I can't help dwelling on Gallipoli,

49 The V1 was an 8m-long pilotless plane powered by a pulse-jet motor and carrying 850kg of explosive with three fuses. They were launched from a fixed ramp, travelled at about 350mph and had a range of 240km. An electrical fuse could be triggered by nose or belly impact. Another fuse was slow acting and mechanical, allowing deeper penetration into the ground. The third fuse was delayed action, set to go off two hours after launch. The purpose of the third fuse was to avoid the risk of this secret weapon being examined by the British. Its time delay was meant to destroy the weapon if a soft landing had not triggered the impact fuses. These fusing systems were very reliable, and almost no dud V1s were recovered.

his attempt to involve the British Army in the Russian Civil War, his treatment of strikers in Britain, his actions in Ireland, India and in the Middle East or – closest to home for me – in Italy. I've often found myself reminding people that it was Churchill's idea of strategy to encourage the USA to make a pre-emptive nuclear strike against the Soviet Union in 1947. I accept entirely that Churchill had his value as an orator during the early part of the war, but please do not tell me he was a great military strategist.

In the autumn of 1946, I was offered a place at the Egham Industrial Rehabilitation Centre in Surrey, one of a network of convalescent and rehabilitation centres for disabled ex-servicemen and women. The Egham Centre offered 'vocational guidance and purposeful training', particularly in building work, shoe repair, retail distribution and manufacturing. I trained as a leather worker, producing men's wallets, among other things.

The Egham Centre consisted of several dozen Army huts surrounding a large Victorian mansion. The house was used exclusively for administrative purposes and as staff quarters. The huts had accommodation for 2,000 wounded ex-servicemen. One of the huts served as a welfare block and included dining rooms and kitchens, a relatively small reading room, which was supposed to be quiet but rarely was, two billiard tables and a gymnasium, which was given over to darts and table tennis.

There wasn't enough space for relaxation and study, and that was a real problem given that a lot of the men attending the unit had lost confidence in themselves because of their disfigurement. The theory was that men might recover their confidence through participation in small informal groups meeting in a relaxed and comfortable atmosphere, but this was simply impossible because of the overcrowding.

Another problem of the unit was that it was not suitable for the needs of so many severely disabled men. Not only were the buildings too far apart, but there were two few toilets and washing facilities. Because I still had significant upper body strength, I was able to cover large distances at a reasonable pace, but one man I knew, who was confined to a wheelchair, couldn't get through the door to the toilets in either the welfare block or the workshops. Every time he wanted to go to the toilet he was forced to go back to his billet. It seemed to me that those with the greatest needs had to suffer the most inconvenience. I couldn't wait to leave Egham, but I had no clear idea what I would do next. I was bitter and resentful about the loss of my youth and prospects. Who wants a man with only one leg?

While I sat at home rueing my misfortune and thinking through the limited range of options available to me, I received a letter inviting me to go to Roehampton to be assessed for the fitting of an artificial leg. I was told that limbless ex-servicemen had no automatic entitlement to artificial appliances.[50] However, the Limb Fitting Centre at Queen Mary's Hospital at Roehampton had begun providing artificial limbs to the wounded ex-servicemen who it was thought might benefit most.[51]

At first, I rejected the offer; it seemed to compound my humiliation. However, my family told me not to be so obstinate and as I began to see other injured servicemen with artificial arms and legs, I slowly began to change my views.

It was explained to me that patients selected for the supply of artificial limbs would receive a programme of instruction at one of the Ministry of Pensions Limb Fitting Centres. There, specialist surgeons and instructors would observe the patient's reactions and capabilities. After the training, the surgeon would advise the Disability Rehabilitation Officer about the patient's physical suitability and capability to benefit from an artificial limb.

I began to read up about artificial limbs as I pondered whether this might be an option for me. I learned that the modern prosthetic leg, jointed and with metal and wood parts, was first developed after the American Civil War, which resulted in 38,000 amputees. James Hanger, who was a Confederate soldier, had patented the 'Hangar Limb' in 1871. It featured hinged joints at both the knee and ankle.

In Britain, most artificial legs were made of willow and leather following a basic design known as the 'Anglesey leg', named after the Marquis of Anglesey. He wore a leg made to this design after he lost one during the Battle of Waterloo in 1815. Earlier versions were also called 'Clapper' legs after the sound the leg made when fully extended.

Wooden prosthetic legs were heavy. They were replaced by lighter, metal versions after design innovations following the Great War, in which 41,000 British servicemen lost one or more limbs. However, the Anglesey limb remained popular well into the twentieth century. It was relatively lightweight and capable of a natural-looking walking movement.

However, everything I read convinced me that an artificial leg was not for me, and I continued with the crutches, as if to publicise to the

50 This entitlement did not arise until the formation of the National Health Service in 1948.

51 Between 3 September 1939 and 30 June 1948, 41,500 artificial limbs were provided, of which 18,300 legs were for service casualties.

world that I didn't want or need any help or support. My father found me an office job in Covent Garden Market, but I knew this wasn't for me. I was desperate for a fresh start.

On Derby Day 1946, my namesake cousin Dinny Neil came up with another daft scheme that seemed too good to be true – and it was. Dinny had read that huge crowds were expected for the Epsom Derby in 1946, the first to be run at Epsom since 1939, after the course had been used as an anti-aircraft battery position during the war. The holiday mood created by the ending of the war meant that up to half a million people were expected, including the King and Queen. Dinny reckoned that it would be easy to set up an unofficial – and unlicensed – bookmaker's pitch up on the Downs and well away from the grandstands where we could pick up bets from the small punters and turn a tidy profit. The scheme sounded exciting, so I readily agreed and on Wednesday, 5 June 1946 we set off by train to Tattenham Corner with a satchel and blackboard.

As predicted, the Downs were packed with people, including many ex-servicemen and their parents in large family groups. I was good at arithmetic and worked out the tissue prices, confident that no matter which horse won we would make a profit. There were seventeen runners with no clear favourite but with horses named Happy Knight, Gulf Stream, Khaled and Fast and Fair, all around 7/1. We noticed that we were picking up lots of small bets for a horse called Airborne, mainly from mothers and sisters of men still resplendent in their RAF uniforms. With the horse being a rank outsider at around 50/1, we lengthened the odds to 66/1 and rubbed our hands together as the money rolled in.

In the initial stages, Airborne was held up and was still well back turning into the straight, with one of the joint favourites, Gulf Stream, in the lead in the last quarter mile. Hardly any of our punters had backed Gulf Stream and we were beginning to count our money as the jockey pulled Airborne wide to produce a sustained run down the centre of the course. He caught Gulf Stream inside the final furlong and won by a length.

The cheers from the groups around us were deafening, but I could see from Dinny's face that we were in trouble. He muttered 'this is going to cost us hundreds.' I looked in the satchel. It contained a lot of money but nowhere near hundreds. 'What are we going to do', I asked him? 'Leg it!' he cried as he scrambled the satchel and blackboard under his arm and ran, leaving me leaning on my crutches.

A group of angry women approached me, waving their handwritten winning betting slips. 'He's gone to get some more money,' I explained apologetically. Then, when the coast was clear, I slipped into the crowd on my crutches, moving as quickly as any two-legged man. When I eventually caught up with Dinny a few days later, it was all I could do to stop myself aping Laurel and Hardy: 'Well, that's another fine mess that you got me into!'

We both agreed that we had been lucky to have escaped with our lives. We vowed that we would never try a stunt like that again.

Chapter 21

SETTLING DOWN

In 1950, the newly elected Conservative government introduced a scheme to give jobs in the Civil Service to wounded ex-servicemen. After a course of lessons, I started work on 13 November 1950, as a typist in the Directorate of Military Intelligence at the War Office in Storey's Gate, just off Whitehall. Although I was very competent at typing, I was very unhappy. This was not the life that I had in mind for myself. I was encouraged to learn shorthand and in 1952 I earned a Certificate in Shorthand at the required speed of 100 words a minute.

It was in that same year that a beautiful but shy young typist joined our pool and was allocated the desk next to mine. Her name was Maisie Budd. I was ten years older than her and acutely conscious of the age gap and my disability. I asked the supervisor of the typing pool to find her another desk, but as there were no others available, we were compelled to tolerate each other. She must have thought me a miserable so and so!

Maisie was born in south London and her mother and father had run a sweetshop in Brixton for a time. Maisie had been evacuated twice during the war to Brighton in 1939 and Barnsley in 1944 and she had had a very disrupted education, but she was highly intelligent and kind. She had studied dressmaking after she left school but had decided to join the War Office in search of a better career.

Over time we started to chat, and after we had finished work on a Saturday morning – and yes, we had to work on Saturdays then – I asked her to come with me to the Lyons' Corner House for lunch. It was not quite as sedate as it may sound; in fact, it used to get very lively in there at times with people dancing on the tables in the middle of the afternoon!

It was not long before I had fallen in love with her gentle ways and her beauty. I was afraid that she would never feel the same way about me, and I was the happiest man on this earth when she told me that she loved me. I decided then that I owed it to her to get an artificial leg.

I went back to Roehampton, and it was explained to me that every amputee had different needs, and those needs were met by highly trained prosthetists who produced sockets that made the connection between the stump and the artificial leg. The procedure was quite comical. A prosthetist came into the room with a bucket full of plaster of Paris. He then asked me to plonk the stump of my leg into the bucket so that he could make a solid replica in plaster. He then asked me to lower the stump back into the bucket to make a socket. He explained that everything depended on how accurately the plaster socket fitted the stump of my leg. The plaster was surprisingly heavy. This was because the plug and stump needed to be as heavy as the original body part it was to replace. Anything else and it just would not feel right, and it would be useless for its purpose.

The prosthetist took the time to explain that stumps are of different volumes, different widths and different lengths. An amputated thigh bone floats about in the soft tissue of the thigh itself, without muscles and ligaments to hold it where it should be, so the socket has to fit closely over the stump and give shape, structure in such a way that the whole thing is made stable, with no more floating about. The socket needs to be not too tight and not too loose: exactly right to hold the stump in a new place, firmly, all the time. Any minor differences would be addressed by a soft woollen sock worn over the stump.

Stability depended on the weight of the rest of the body and how that comes down on to the stump. Bone that has been cut through can't take weight, so the socket has to be designed to take the weight of the body and distribute it back to areas that still have soft and hard tissue intact. This means the weight is moved through the socket to areas that can carry it, such as the hips and pelvis. In my case, the socket had to go high up the leg, almost to the hip, to provide the support to my soft tissue and what was left of my muscles.

I read later that even today, the best computer scanner is not a match for an experienced prosthetist with an artist's eye and a set of fine files to reshape carefully until the fit is as good as it can be. I'm not sure how true it is, but my prosthetist told me that anyone who knows how they work can tell who built which model, 'like telling a Michelangelo from a Bernini'.

I cannot say that I took to my artificial leg immediately. I had to undergo hours of training with the prosthetist and a physiotherapist learning how to walk on two legs again. However, in due course, I mastered it, and I soon began to wonder why I had been so silly for so long.

On 27 March 1954 Maisie and I were married at St Margaret's Church at Lee Park, near Blackheath, and we went on honeymoon to Brighton, staying in a bed and breakfast guest house in Queen's Road recommended by Maisie's friend Doris. After our marriage we moved in with her parents at 17 Lee Park.

Just two months after we were married, Maisie fell pregnant, but sadly she miscarried. We were absolutely delighted, therefore, to get the news just a few weeks later that Maisie was pregnant again. Our daughter Mary was born on 3 March 1955, but I will never forget the day that we were told that Mary was born with spina bifida. In the 1950s, the survival rate for infants with spina bifida was quite low due to complications such as infections and hydrocephalus (fluid build-up in the brain). Tragically, Mary died at just six days old on Wednesday, 9 March 1955.

Maisie took Mary's death very hard, and we both agreed that we needed a fresh start. We were still living in Lee Park and the prospect of starting afresh in a new council house outside London was extremely exciting. We had heard about plans to build a new estate at Merstham and I was aware that the Ministry of Pensions had an office just down the road in Redhill. It sounded like a perfect opportunity for us.

The first plans for an estate at Merstham had been lodged in 1948 but were bitterly opposed by the local borough and county council and numerous letters of objection appeared in the local paper. Attempts were made to get the land designated as a Green Belt Preservation area, but the LCC overruled these objections and obtained a compulsory purchase order in 1949. Building work commenced in 1950.

The houses of the new estate were planned in an attractive modern style from decent quality materials. They all had bathrooms and small gardens, with children's recreation areas and green spaces. Land was designated for three churches: Church of England, Roman Catholic and Baptist, five new schools, a parade of shops, two pubs, a cinema, a health centre, community centre and library. It reflected the utopian ideal of the day to create a self-contained community with everything that its inhabitants could need within easy walking distance. The surrounding area was still essentially rural with several small farms and pasture dotted with venerable oak trees. To us, it seemed idyllic.

On 27 May 1955, Maisie and I moved into a brand-new maisonette in Chilmark Gardens in Merstham. The maisonette was well-designed and close to the bus route and local shops. It was also just a couple of hundred yards from open countryside and we loved walking out for picnics or the occasional drink in the *Warwick Arms,* an isolated rural pub in the nearby hamlet of Warwick Wold. Just four days later

I started a new job as a clerical officer in the Ministry of Pensions at North Street, Redhill.

My young nephew Danny was a frequent visitor, sometimes on his own, but on one occasion with his latest girlfriend. He loved going for walks with me across the woods and fields around Merstham but he wasn't so keen on the local youths who hung around outside the coffee bar in Portland Drive. He called them the 'Merstham Cow-boys'.

Our joy was confirmed when we learned that Maisie was pregnant again. Our beautiful daughter Sharon Kathleen was born on 8 December 1956. She was wonderful: happy and healthy, or so it seemed. When Sharon was just 14 months old, Maisie fell pregnant again and our first son John Terence was born fit and healthy on 11 November 1958. For an abbreviated period, our happiness was unbounded. John was developing well and Sharon's first report from her nursery confirmed that she was making substantial progress in her play and interaction with others. Her nursery report concluded: 'Sharon tries hard to co-operate in all that's asked of her. A carefree disposition.'

The maisonette was too small for us now, so we applied for, and were granted, a transfer to a two-bedroom house in Portland Drive, opposite the parade of shops. We became good friends with our neighbours, the Millards, who had children of a similar age to Sharon and John. It was perfect.

Because I had learned to drive in the Army, I was never required to take a normal driving test, and I bought a car under a Ministry of Pensions scheme for war disabled, which provided for hand controls to be added to a car purchased by the pensioner. The hand controls were operated by pulling a lever fitted to the left-hand side of the steering wheel that controlled the accelerator. The brake was controlled by pushing a separate vertical lever attached to the floor. The car could still be driven using the pedals, as these remained in place. That first car was a beautiful, red Singer Super 10 but it wasn't very reliable and I replaced it with a second-hand black Ford Popular from Wadham Stringer in Redhill.

But then, a series of dark shadows appeared in our lives. My father fell ill and died on 8 April 1960 before he had really got to know Sharon and John. He only visited Merstham once. That one visit occurred in the year he died at bluebell time. We took him and my mother out for a drive, and he asked us to stop the car so he could see the bluebells. I will never forget him lying there in that beautiful glade staring up at the clear blue skies in a state of perfect bliss.

At around the same time, we noticed that although Sharon appeared to be perfectly normal, she was falling behind other children of a similar age in terms of her speech. She had quickly learned to say 'Mama' and 'Dadda' but did not seem to be adding to her vocabulary. At first, we were not unduly concerned, but as the weeks and months went by, it became increasingly clear that something was wrong. She began to show less eye contact and have no interest in toys. She was slow to start crawling and she began to wring her hands.

At first, we did not think these things were significant, but by the time she was three she had lost purposeful hand skills and had not developed any spoken language. Her uncoordinated hand movements became more pronounced, and when she walked she seemed to sway.

We talked things over with Dr Reginald Redd, our family GP, a kindly man with a permanent twinkle in his eye who had flown Spitfires during the war. He agreed to refer Sharon to a specialist at Redhill General Hospital. There then followed a never-ending string of hospital visits and tests, none of which provided us with a clear diagnosis or prognosis. We were eventually told that Sharon had been classified as mentally handicapped, but nothing could be done for her. We were offered a place at Royal Earlswood Hospital, a home for the mentally handicapped just south of Redhill, but we vowed we would always care for her at home, no matter what it took.

It was not until many years later that Sharon's condition was diagnosed as Rett syndrome (after Andreas Rett, a paediatrician in Austria) caused by a mutation of the X2 chromosome and which occurs almost exclusively in girls.

In the summer of 1963, we learned that Maisie was pregnant again and our second son Michael Dennis was born on 18 March 1963 in Redhill General Hospital. However, immediately after he was born, we learned that the doctors had detected cancer in Maisie's cervix. The only option was for surgery to remove the growth. Dr Redd found a place for Sharon at a day centre for the handicapped in Caterham. John, who was not yet at primary school, was placed in a day nursery in Cromwell Road so that I could carry on working. Maisie stayed in hospital for around six weeks until she was eventually given the all clear.

When Maisie came out of hospital I was determined to make things better for our family. First, I traded in our Ford Popular that John's friends branded 'an old banger'. I bought a much more desirable two-tone maroon Ford Anglia from the same garage in Redhill. However, I didn't keep it long because in late 1963 I learned that the Ministry of Health was providing war pensioners with Morris Mini Minor cars.

So, I sold the beloved Ford Anglia and became the proud user – but not owner – of a brand new, blue, 850cc Mini Mark 1;[52] the trendiest car on the British roads. Although it was smaller and less comfortable than the Anglia, we loved it. I kept the Mini until 1970, when it was replaced by a Morris Minor that was modified for my use by Reselco of King Street, Hammersmith.

In 1964, Bob Craig, a neighbour in Merstham invited me to join the newly formed Redhill branch of the Disabled Drivers Association, which met in the South-East Surrey Spastics Centre in Frenches Road, Redhill. In addition to organising social events, the Association also provided its members with special number plates bearing the signage 'Disabled Driver – No Hand Signals'. I declined the invitation. Although I liked and respected Bob, I had no desire to mix with other disabled drivers, or to remind other road users of my disability.

We loved taking Sharon, Michael and John out for daytrips. Our favourite outing was to the recreation ground at Ticehust. I chose this as it had swings, a roundabout and a slide for John and plenty of space with few other people around so Sharon could wander freely.

Desperate to take the children on a summer holiday but short of money to pay for the holiday camp holidays that were being enjoyed by John's friends, I was delighted when the owner of the greengrocer shop in Endsleigh Road offered us the use of their bungalow, Sunblest, at Pebble Road, Pevensey. The rent was a very generous £10 for two weeks in August.

We all fell in love with Sunblest. It was located right on the beach at Pevensey Bay next to a children's home. The next-door neighbour was Maurice Amos, a builder from Emlyn Road, Redhill. The bungalow was basic, with bare floorboards and no television or radio, but we were incredibly happy and contented there. Maisie's parents came down with us on that first weekend on 1964 and my father-in-law and I spent that first Saturday line fishing off the beach. In the evenings we all bundled into his Austin A40 and drove out to *The Lamb* at Hooe and *The Horseshoe* at Hailsham. We returned to Sunblest every year until 1970.

On 5 June 1967, I was promoted to executive officer and transferred to the DHSS Regional Office at Sutherland House in Sutton. I was

52 The Mini bore a small plate on the engine that reminded everyone that the car remained 'Government Property'.

happy there and our annual holiday to Sunblest was one of the best times of our life. The weather was perfect and the boys made friends with the family who were staying in Amos' bungalow next door. Low tides occurred in the early mornings and early evenings and these times were spent walking on the fine sands. Although I was still conscious of my artificial leg, I went out in the late evenings and swam in the sea on the incoming tide.

However, as summer turned into autumn, we began to find Sharon increasingly difficult to manage. She was now increasingly irritable and angry and would burst into bitter, unceasing tears. Her distress was palpable, and it took its toll on Maisie.

In the spring of 1968 Maisie and I decided that, despite our earlier vow, we could not take Sharon on our forthcoming holiday to Seaton in Devon and that we needed to place her into respite care at Royal Earlswood. We both felt treacherous and although we tried to put a brave face on it for John and Michael, Maisie cried every night and sometimes through the day. We felt like traitors.

On our return from holiday, we picked up Sharon from Royal Earlswood Hospital on Sunday morning in late June. I will never forget that bleak, unhappy place. We were not allowed to go to the ward where Sharon had been staying but had to wait in the gloomy, cavernous reception while a nurse fetched her for us. The wait seemed interminable. When she finally emerged holding the hand of a stern-faced nurse, we saw immediately that she was wearing none of the nice clothes that she had gone in there with. Instead, she had an ill-fitting, hand-knitted jumper, a frayed grey skirt and odd socks. Maisie cried and cried.

We persevered with Sharon at home for the next few months, but it became increasingly difficult as Sharon's uncontrolled outbursts became more frequent. She also started to have epileptic fits that were hugely unsettling, even though she usually recovered quickly.

It was in July 1968 that the dam burst. We had taken Sharon, John and Michael to Dunorlan Park at Tunbridge Wells. It was a hot day, and the park was crowded with families enjoying the fine weather. Sharon was unusually distressed with constant handwringing and crying and people were staring as if we were maltreating her. There was nothing about her physical appearance to suggest that she was different, so why was she so distressed? We decided to return home but as we walked back towards the car, she burst out with a loud cry of 'Mama'. It was the first word that she had spoken since she was three and it was the very last word that she ever spoke.

With our annual holiday to Sunblest looming we decided that, for the sake of John and Michael, that Sharon should go into Royal Earlswood permanently. We were assured, and we managed to convince ourselves, that our first impressions of Royal Earlswood were unfair and that it was not as bad as it seemed. We were told that Sharon's clothes were mislaid because they were not marked with her name and that all we had to do was to apply name tags. We were told that the stern nurse was caring and kind and that although the reception might seem unwelcoming, the wards were cheerful, bright and clean. Most importantly, we were told that Sharon was happy there and could be properly cared for should she have another fit. We gave in for the sake of the boys.

In 1970, while on holiday in Pevensey Bay we went to Hastings on a day trip, and stopped off at Combe Haven Caravan Park. Maisie's mother was staying with us, and she told us about how much enjoyment she had got from owning a caravan. In the car back to Pevensey we stopped at the traffic lights at Cooden Beach and out of the blue Maisie's mother offered to lend us the £560 to buy a Bluebird Calypso caravan. It was an act of generosity that gave us endless pleasure over the following thirty-seven years.

On 1 July 1974 I was promoted to higher executive officer and became manager of the DHSS office at Caterham with around two dozen staff in an old Victorian house in Godstone Road.

In 1975 a new Mobility Allowance was created to meet the extra costs associated with mobility for disabled people. Alongside this the Labour government also created Motability, a scheme that bought cars from British manufacturers, adapted them for disabled people and leased them to claimants in lieu of a cash payment. Under this scheme, I leased a brand-new Ford Escort Mark II.

As I entered my 50s, and some thirty years after my wounding, I began to suffer from intense, relentless, phantom leg pains; the sensation that my amputated right leg was still attached to my body. As I grew older, the condition became chronic and resistant to all but the strongest drugs and I became addicted to Diazepam (Valium), sometimes taking up to twelve tablets in a single night. Dr Redd explained to me that Valium sedates the central nervous system, but the brain is very clever and will respond to Valium by learning to tolerate it, which means that it no longer works as well. This leads to people taking a larger dose to experience the same release. Valium also has a long half-life, which means it stays in the person's body for a long time. As a result, I frequently came close to overdosing, leaving me debilitated for days.

In the 1970s I was prescribed Tramadol and sometimes the pain was so severe that I would take nine, ten or more tablets in a short period, causing indigestion, constipation and, worst of all, night terrors that would leave me quivering in a cold sweat. The tablets became a psychological crutch, and I became anxious and depressed if ever I did not have the tablets close at hand. Despite a great deal of research into phantom limb pain, there is still no clear consensus as to its cause. Whatever is behind it, the pain was real, persistent and relentless: a legacy of the events on that mountainside in 1943.

I suffered most in the harsh winters of the early 1970s when snow lingered and pavements turned slippery with compacted slush. I parked my car in a council garage in Taynton Drive some 400 yards from our house in Weldon Way for the simple reason that it often would not start if left out in the open. The walk to the garage was treacherous underfoot and, on several occasions, I slipped and fell. On one occasion in the winter of 1972, I fell so heavily on the cold, hard ground that I damaged my artificial leg. I had to go to Roehampton to get it repaired. After that, I would often ask Maisie or John to walk with me, leaning heavily on their shoulders to maintain my balance.

After that fall, I decided to approach the British Legion to ask them to help me purchase a 3ft strip of waste land from the grounds of St Teresa's Catholic church to enable me to build a garage next door to my house. The British Legion refused immediately, stating that they could not get involved in property disputes. In my experience this was typical. There was always some reason why they could never provide any practical help. I then decided to make a direct approach to Father Stonehill, the Roman Catholic priest of St Teresa's church.

Father Stonehill listened without showing any obvious sympathy or understanding. He asked if I was a Catholic and when I said that I was, he corrected me with the words 'a lapsed Catholic'. However, he agreed to refer the request to the Diocesan Secretary for the Diocese of Arundel. Some weeks passed by until I received a formal letter from solicitors asking £100 for a lease for the 3ft strip and setting out several conditions, including a requirement that any garage be placed in the rear garden of my house rather than alongside the house. It would have meant losing my beautiful back garden. I rejected the offer and appealed to the solicitors to show a little Christian charity. My request was ignored, thereby demolishing any lingering allegiance both to the British Legion or the Roman Catholic church.

I used to visit my mother and my Aunt Flo in Betterton Streetevery Sunday morning, picking up my brother Bert on the way from his flat in Lambeth. I bought my mother a budgie that she taught to talk in a Drury Lane accent that mirrored hers. I'll never forget his comical, repeated babbling of 'Who's a lovely, bubbly baby'! My mother suffered increasingly bad health as she grew older and had to have her arm amputated in 1972.

In August 1974, my mother died while we were away on holiday in Wales. My sister Nora had made several attempts to contact me but in the days before mobile phones she had no way of getting a message through. The phone rang the moment that we walked back into the house after the long drive from Camrose, near Haverfordwest. At first, Nora tried to soften the news by telling me merely that my mother was seriously ill in hospital, but she couldn't keep up the pretence and she burst out that my mother had died. I unpacked the car with tears in my eyes that I had not been with her when she passed.

To add to our unhappiness, Maisie then suffered another cruel blow when she was told that the cancer had returned and that she needed a hysterectomy. Fortunately, John and Michael were now at school and Sharon was resident at Royal Earlswood, so we coped without needing any external help. After convalescence, Maisie made a full recovery, and our lives resumed.

We had many happy times in the late 1970s and 1980s. We enjoyed our lives immensely and had settled into a routine of bringing Sharon home every weekend. Although we never grew to love Royal Earlswood, we recognised that most – but by no means all – of the staff were doing their best in a depressing building and limited resources. So little was understood then about the causes of a mental impairment like Sharon had.

Two of the other inmates on Sharon's ward were Nerissa and Katherine Bowes-Lyon, who were maternal first cousins of Queen Elizabeth II. The two women had been air-brushed out of existence in *Burke's Peerage*, which recorded that Nerissa and Katherine had died in 1940 and 1961 respectively. *The Sun* newspaper claimed to have discovered their existence, but this was common knowledge within Royal Earlswood. Although both women were aware of their Royal connections and took a keen interest in Royal ceremonies on television, the sisters were never visited by any member of the Bowes-Lyon or Royal Family, despite their aunt, the Queen Mother, being a Patron of Mencap (a charity for people with learning disabilities). They never even received birthday or Christmas cards. When Nerissa and Katherine died, none of their family attended the funeral and their graves were marked with plastic tags and a serial number. It was some years until the truth came out.

In 1985, John told us that he intended to marry his girlfriend Jaqueline Wake, whom he had met at work. We were delighted as we both liked Jackie very much. However, on the Monday before the wedding date of 20 April 1985, the phone rang at 7 a.m. Instinctively apprehensive about any phone call at that time of the morning, I saw Maisie listen in silence until she gasped 'Oh, no!' Sharon had died unexpectedly in the night. Our poor, dear helpless daughter taken from us on what we were hoping would be a happy week.

John drove us down to Royal Earlswood, where we were taken to a side room and shown Sharon lying lifeless, peaceful but still warm. How could our precious daughter have left us? We were told later that she had died of an epileptic fit during the night and that nothing could have been done to save her. However, Maisie and I both doubted that. If she had been home with us, at least we would have been with her. She would not have died alone in that gruesome hospital ward.

We had little time to grieve, with the wedding of our first son in just five days' time. We decided quickly that the wedding must go ahead and so it did at St John the Divine church in Selsdon. I will never cease to be in awe of Maisie's resilience and strength that she was able to bear this.

As I look back on my life, I study a balance sheet of many credits and debits. I am grateful to my parents, my sister and brothers. I also appreciate my good fortune in surviving my wounds. Most of all I am grateful for the gift of my wonderful wife and children. Overall, I have been a very lucky man.

And yet, Maisie and I saw more than our fair share of tragedy. I think constantly about the loss of my daughters Mary and Sharon. Why were they born with these conditions? I think of the cruel, premature, death of my brother Jimmy and the fact that I could not be there when my mother died. Selfishly, I also remember the loss of my leg and the discomfort, constant pain and physical restrictions that my wounds caused me. I was earnestly devout in my younger days, and I do not think I ever doubted the existence of God, but I never understood how a loving God could have allowed such things to happen. Perhaps, there are things that we are not supposed to understand.

I have thought a lot about the nature of bravery, patriotism and heroism. I always found it a cruel irony that I was sent to fight in Italy of all places. I knew many Italian and German families and liked them well enough. Is it bravery to slit a throat or thrust a bayonet into someone just because they come from another country? Is it patriotic to excuse war crimes committed by your own side? Is it heroic to rain down bombs and missiles on innocent civilians far, far away? Why do we pretend that all servicemen are heroes? I was not brave. I was not patriotic, and I certainly was never a hero.

In 1980, Maisie and I took our first holiday abroad: a two-week stay in Sorrento, with a pre-booked pilgrimage to Monte Cassino. It was not a return visit because I never got that far in 1943! One morning at breakfast, I was jostled by a German man of about my age who had the benefit of all his limbs. I realised instantly that he was probably revisiting the Italian battlefields too. We glared at each other across the buffet, until a flicker of recognition passed between us, and he nodded his head in a gesture that could have passed for a salute. It crossed my mind immediately that he might possibly have been the German soldier who fired the mortar shell that maimed me all those years ago. We continued filling our plates and I never saw him again.

I never collected my medals. I never wanted them. And I never joined the British Legion or any other ex-servicemen's organisation. It was not that I did not respect my fellow servicemen, it was just that I saw no merit in continually harping on about the war. You can keep your eulogies, your public services of remembrance, your poppies and marching bands. They mean nothing to me. I have seen war, and I hate everything about it.

EPILOGUE

My father, Dennis Joseph Patrick Neil, died of cancer of the oesophagus on 22 July 1997 after an illness that was diagnosed less than twelve months before. Right up until the end he was convinced that fate would protect him as it had done before and that he would make a full recovery. He jumped at the opportunity for respite care at a hospice in Caterham, believing that this would speed his return to health. When the consultant broke the news that he would not recover, it broke him and he begged to be allowed to go home.

His last few weeks were grim, with frequent overwhelming nightmares and hallucinations. On one occasion his terror of an imaginary thickening and enveloping grey cloud caused him to fall helpless on the floor beside his bed. He had a clock on the bedroom wall that caught a reflection from the window that gave it an appearance of an oriental face. He told me one day: 'I'm glad I can see that Chinese girl, because all the time I can see her, I know I'm still here.' Then, the day came when he could no longer see the face.

He deteriorated rapidly towards the end and the family gathered at his bedside on my mother's birthday. He died at 10.50 the following morning, as if he didn't want to spoil her day.

I am eternally grateful that my father and I were such firm friends and that I was able to spend so much time with him over many a lunchtime pint. He lived a life that was full, and I think he was always appreciative of the fact that he had so many years after his near-death experience in the field hospital in Naples.

He held no lingering bitterness towards the Italians and Germans, or Churchill and the Allied commanders. I think he regarded Churchill as the right man for the times in 1940 and that no other British politician could have rallied the British people or forge the friendship with Roosevelt that ultimately won the war, but no more than that.

My father was a man of great sensitivity and compassion. A life-long socialist and an admirer of Michael Foot, but also a keen reader of the *Daily Telegraph*. He loved boxing, horse racing and snooker but he was also an avid reader of novels, short stories and non-fiction. I still have the very last book he read – a copy of the complete short stories of his favourite author, Ernest Hemingway. He loved Ireland and all things Irish, but he supported England at football. He believed in social justice and the welfare state, and he was proud of his position in the DHSS. He had no time for military pomp and circumstance, but he was always grateful for his war pension and the support he received from Roehampton.

My father was a complex man. Even now I am not sure that I fully understand him, but I'm not sure that I need to. I just hope that I have done him justice in this book.

APPENDIX: THE MYTH OF THE BALLAD OF THE D-DAY DODGERS

So, after all that, how did the brave men who served in the Italian campaign become known as the D-Day Dodgers? As with much else associated in the Second World War, the mythology has outgrown the truth.

Here are the lyrics of the D-Day Dodgers song that was sung to the tune of 'Lilli Marleen':

We're the D-Day Dodgers, way off in Italy
Always on the vino, always on the spree;
Eighth Army scroungers and their tanks,
We live in Rome, among the Yanks.
We are the D-Day Dodgers, way out in Italy.

We landed in Salerno, a holiday with pay,
The Jerries brought the bands out to greet us on the way.
Showed us the sights and gave us tea,
We all sang songs, the beer was free
To welcome D-Day Dodgers to sunny Italy.

Naples and Cassino were taken in our stride,
We didn't go to fight there, we went just for the ride.
Anzio and Sangro were just names,
We only went to look for dames,
The artful D-Day Dodgers, way out in Italy.

On our way to Florence we had a lovely time.
We ran a bus to Rimini right through the Gothic Line.
On to Bologna we did go,
Then we all had a paddle in the Po.
For we are the D-Day Dodgers, out here in Italy.

Dear Lady Astor, you think you know a lot,
Standing on a platform, talking tommyrot.
You're England's sweetheart and her pride.
We think your mouth's too bleeding wide.
That's from your D-Day Dodgers, in sunny Italy.

Look around the mountains, in the mud and rain,
You'll find the scattered crosses, there's some that have no name.
Heartbreak and toil and suffering gone,
The boys beneath them slumber on.
They are the D-Day Dodgers who stay in Italy.

The term, 'D-Day Dodger' was attributed to Conservative MP Nancy Astor. The story goes that she used the phrase in a speech in the House of Commons, implying that the men who could not join in the Normandy landings were taking it easy in sunny Italy.

The second reason why Lady Astor is remembered today is as the butt of one of Churchill's most famous rejoinders. After she told him: 'If I were married to you, I'd put poison in your coffee', he is reputed to have replied, 'If I were married to you, I'd drink it.' It is an amusing story; reinforcing, as it does, the caricatures of Churchill as an erudite witty statesman – 'the greatest Englishman' and Lady Astor as an example of an uppity but ignorant American. However, both stories are untrue.

Churchill's speeches, letters and published works contain millions of words and so it is easy to put witty remarks in his mouth that he never uttered, but the 'poison' gag was not invented by Churchill.[53] It was used by F.E. Smith (Lord Birkenhead) in 1946 with reference to Bessie Braddock, the long-serving Labour MP for Liverpool. However, Lord Birkenhead didn't invent the joke either. It first featured in a New York newspaper in 1899 and was attributed to the American actor Marshal Pinckney Wilder. The joke was also used by W.C. Fields, Groucho Marx and George Bernard Shaw.

So, who was Lady Astor? She was born Nancy Witcher Langhorne in Danville, Virginia, the eighth of eleven children born to railroad tycoon Chiswell Dabney. Her first marriage, to socialite Robert Gould Shaw II, ended in divorce. She then moved to England and married

53 Richard Langworth, the editor of four books of authenticated Churchill quotations, estimates that there are at least eighty famous sayings attributed to Churchill that were not his. This is fortunate for authors and journalists, because Churchill's estate charges a licence fee for the reuse of almost everything he published, including his speeches.

American-born Englishman Waldorf Astor in 1906. After he entered the House of Lords, she stood for Parliament and won her husband's former seat of Plymouth Sutton in 1919, becoming the first woman to sit as an MP in the House of Commons. During her time in Parliament, Nancy Astor was an advocate for temperance, welfare, education reform and women's rights. She was also an ardent anti-Catholic, anti-communist, and anti-Semite, but she was primarily a Conservative – not an opponent of Churchill – and he was a regular attendee at her dinner parties at Cliveden.

The earliest reference to the term 'D-Day Dodger' occurred in October 1944, when a correspondent (who signed off as 'A Desert Rat, RAF') wrote to the *Citizen*, a short-lived publication that primarily focused on issues concerning the working class and social justice: 'a few days ago, I met a couple of Gloucester lads who told us that the people at home were calling us D-Day Dodgers'.

Four months later (on 22 February 1945) the term turned up again in a letter that appeared in the *Daily Mirror* from Lance Corporal F. Bryant, Central Mediterranean Force:

> We hear that in Blighty we here are called the D-Day Dodgers. We're going to be very plain spoke about this. Our telephone is ringing all day with people who have been in a pub, or a cinema and have been told by someone who overheard some-body else tell someone they knew that their friend from the Mediterranean had been called a D-Day Dodger. Tell any person who says that that he (or she) is a liar; and if he says he did hear it said, then tell him he's a damned liar. It has never been said. The entire thing is a story on a par with the tale of the Yank who asked in a pub for a drink, 'and quicker than the British Army got out of France.' It never happened; neither has the term D-Day Dodger been used. We get round a bit, and we should have been the first to hear it.

By February 1945 the term was in widespread use. So much so, that Lady Astor was moved to write to the service magazine, *Union Jack*, to offer her defence and explanation of her role in the promulgation of this term:

> I have just heard that you and your men are indignant about my calling you D-Day Dodgers. None of you is as hurt or indignant as I am. On December 12 I received an airgraph signed 'D-Day Dodgers' and I thought they had nick-named their particular company with that name, so I wrote back. 'Dear D-Day Dodgers.' And from that little friendly letter, the damn-fool story has circulated. (*Daily Mirror*, 27 February 1945).

This account was confirmed by Lieutenant Colonel H. Gill in a letter to the *Bedfordshire Times and Standard* dated 6 April 1945, in which he quotes the *8th Army News*. However, there was no mention of Lady Astor in the original lyrics that appeared in the version published in the *Brechin Advertiser* (and other local and regional papers) on 24 April 1945.

The first reference to Lady Astor appeared in a nine-verse version of the lyrics published in the *Weekly News* dated 6 July 1945; two months after VE Day. The letter was written by 'two Runcornian' members of the Central Mediterranean Force who claimed: 'We here have composed this little ditty about ourselves.' It has many minor differences to the April 1945 version, and it also contains these two additional verses:

Oh! Please Lady Astor, listen, dear to us.
You're the forces sweetheart, the nation's pride
But your pretty mouth opens much too wide
We know we're the D-Day Dodgers, out in Italy.

Now the war is over, the battle has been won
We'll get back to Blighty, years after all the fun
And when we get back, forgotten we'll be
For we're only the lads of the Eighth Army.
We were D-Day Dodgers back in Italy.

The *Weekly News* article provides more information about the provenance of the song, confirming that it should be sung to the tune of 'Lili Marleen' that was composed by Norbert Schultze in 1938 and recorded by Lale Andersen in 1939. It was often heard by British soldiers serving in North Africa and it came to be adopted as a theme song of the 8th Army and the 6th Armoured Division.[54]

There were several subsequent but slightly different versions published in the British national and local press in 1945. There was also a Canadian version. Some sources attribute the song to the Scottish poet and folklorist, Hamish Henderson who included it in his *Ballads of World War II*, which was published privately in 1947.[55] Henderson was

54 In early 1942 Lale Anderson recorded the song in English, with lyrics translated by Norman Baillie-Stewart. In 1941 Radio Belgrade became the German forces' radio station, with transmissions heard throughout Europe and the Mediterranean. Karl-Heinz Reintgen, the German officer in charge of the station, played the song frequently.

55 It was published privately by the Caledonian Press under the fictitious 'Lilli Marlene' imprint because of the ripe language that Henderson used and his refusal to bowdlerise the lyrics that he had recorded.

a respected British Army officer who served as an intelligence officer in Egypt, Libya, Tunisia and Italy. While in Italy, he wrote the first of his great songs, 'The Highland Division's Farewell to Italy' and composed the pipe march that was played at the Anzio beachhead. However, Henderson never claimed the 'D-Day Dodgers' as his own. He always attributed it to 'Anonymous'.

There is an intriguing claim made by the respected folklorist Roy Palmer,[56] who attributed the lyrics to Lance Sergeant Harry Roland (Jack) Pynn (1913–86). Pynn was born in Weedon Bec in Northamptonshire, where his father was factory foreman and an amateur light comedian with the Weedon Pierrots before the war. Harry had worked as a van driver before volunteering for the Army in 1940. To his disappointment, he was posted to the Army Fire Service in England. However, in September 1942, he was posted to North Africa and he served in Sicily and the assaults on the Viktor Line, Barbara Line, Winter Line, Monte Cassino and the Trasimene Line. It is not clear how Palmer identified Pynn as the author of the lyrics.

So, whether the lyrics were written by 'two Runcornians', a distinguished Scottish poet or a Northamptonshire fireman is now lost in the mists of history. But perhaps it doesn't matter. Perhaps, it was that rare thing; an authentic, anonymous, twentieth-century English folk song.

56 Roy Palmer (10 February 1932–26 February 2015) wrote more than thirty books on folklore and folk song. He attributed 'The D-Day Dodgers' to Harry Prynn in *What a Lovely War! British Soldiers' Songs from the Boer War to the Present Day*. London: Michael Joseph, p.227.

BIBLIOGRAPHY

Adelman, R.H. (1968). *Rome Fell Today*. London: Leslie Frewin.

Air Ministry AIR 29/512. (1940). AIR 29/512. Manchester: None.

Allen, W.L. (1978). *Anzio, Edge of Disaster*. New York: Elsevier-Dutton.

Annussek, G.A. (2005). *Hitler's Raid to Save Mussolini: the most infamous commando operation of World War II*. Cambridge, MA: Da Capo Press.

Battistelli, P. P. (2023). *The Winter Campaign In Italy 1943*. New York: Osprey Publishing Ltd.

Brooke, A. (2001). *War Diaries, 1939–1945: Field Marshal Lord Alanbrooke*. San Francisco: Berkeley: University of California Press. Originally pub. 1957.

Bruce, G. (1987). *Second Front Now!: the road to D-Day*. London: McDonald & Jane.

Bryant, A. (1957). *The Turn of the Tide 1939–1943*. New York: Doubleday.

Buckingham, W.F. (2008). *Paras*. Stroud: Tempus.

Butcher, H.C. (1946). *Three Years with Eisenhower*. New York: Heinemann.

Churchill, W.S. (1929). *The World Crisis*. New York: Charles Scribner.

Churchill, W.S. (1948). *The Second World War, Volume VI*. London: Houghton and Mifflin.

Clark, L. (2006). *Anzio: The Friction of War. Italy and the Battle for Rome 1944*. London: Headline Publishing Group.

Clark, M.W. (1954). *Calculated Risk*. New York: Harper & Brothers.

Collier, R. (1983). *The Freedom Road 1944–45*. New York: Athenaeum.

Crew, F. (1956). *The Army Medical Services: Campaigns*. London: HMSO.

Daily Herald. (11 January 1919).

Daily Herald. (11 August 1922). The Felon's Cap, p.2.

Daily Herald. (16 April 1941). Soho Waiter was a Paratroop Hero, p.1.

Daily Telegraph. (3 November 1942). In Memory of a Hero, p.4.

Devine, R.A. (1966). *Roosevelt and World War II*. Baltimore: John Hopkins Press.

Dundee Courier, The Covent Garden Strike. (1924, September 25), p.4.

Eiler, K. (1987). *Wedemeyer on War and Peace*. New York: Hanover Press.

Eisenhower, J.S. (2012). *Soldiers and Statesmen: reflections on leadership*. Columbia: Missouri University Press.

Este, C. (24 March 2017). *The Man Who Knew No Fear: General Lucian K. Truscott*. Retrieved from History Net, www.historynet.com/man-knew-no-fear-general-lucian-k-truscott

Gelb, N. (1992). *Desperate Venture.* New York: William Morrow.

Gilbert, M. (1966). *Winston Churchill's Road to Victory.* Boston: Houghton Mifflin.

Gilbert, M. (2005). *Churchill and America.* New York: Free Press.

Gillon, S.M. (2011). *Pearl Harbor: FDR leads the nation into war.* New York: Basic Books.

Guingand, F.de (1947). *Operation Victory.* London: Hodder & Stoughton.

Hamilton, N. (2011). Churchill's Blunder: Anzio. *Defense Media Network.*

Hampshire Telegraph & Post. (3 April 1936). Hitler's Peace Plan.

Harris, J.M. (2009). *American Soldiers and POW Killings in the European Theatre of World War 2.* San Marcos, TX: University of Texas.

Hart, P. (1998). *The I.R.A. and its Enemies: violence and community in Cork, 1916–1923.* Oxford: Clarendon Press.

Higgins, T. (1957). *Winston Churchill and the Second Front, 1940–1943.* New York: Oxford University Press.

HMSO. (6 June 1944). House of Commons debates. *Hansard House of Commons debates, volume 400,* Columns 1207–11.

Holland, J. (2008). *Italy's Sorrow.* London: Harper Collins.

Holland, J. (2023). *The Savage Storm: The Battle for Italy 1943.* London: Bantam.

Ickes, H.L. (1955). *The Secret Diary of Harold L. Ickes.* New York: Simon & Schuster.

Irish Central. (24 March 2024). On This Day Winston Churchill Ordered the Black & Tans into Ireland in 1920.

Irish Times, The Covent Garden Strike. (20 August 1920), p.8.

Knight, N. (Cincinnati). *Churchill: the greatest Briton unmasked.* 2008: David & Charles.

Kuroski, J. (2016). *The Worst War Crimes committed by the US during World War II.* Internet: Internet Archive.

Lewis, N. (1978). *Naples '44.* London: Collins.

Liverpool Daily Post. (9 December 1939). Answer to the Heinkels, p.7.

Liverpool Echo. (20 July 1943). Massing at Messina, p.4.

Londonderry Sentinel. (12 July 1932). Irish Republican Army Appeal to Orangemen, p.2.

Majdalany, F. (1957). *Cassino: Portrait of a Battle.* London: Longmans, Green & Co.

Mawdsley, E. (2012). *December 1941: twelve days that began a world war.* Newhaven: Yale University Press.

Meehan, P. (1995). *The Unnecessary War: Whitehall and the German resistance to Hitler.* London: Sinclair Stephenson.

Merlin, G. (2008). General Francis Tuker and the Bombing of Monte Cassino. *BBC's WW2 People's War.*

Miller, T. (1852). *Picturesque Sketches of London, Past and Present.* London: Office of the National Illustrated Library.

Moran, C.M. (1966). *Churchill, taken from the diaries of Lord Moran; the struggle for survival, 1940–1965.* Boston: Houghton Mifflin.

Morin, R. (1965). *Churchill: Portrait of Greatness.* Englewood Cliffs: Prentice-Hall.
Nisbet, R.A. (1988). *Roosevelt and Stalin: the Failed Courtship.* London: Simon & Schuster.
North, J. (1962). *The Alexander Memoirs.* London: Cassell.
Nottingham Evening Post. Mutiny Fiasco. (1919, May 12), p.1.
Nottingham and Midland Catholic News. (1921, June 4). Little Girl Killed for a Bet. Looter and Sharpshooter. Murderous Act by Black and Tans in Kerry.
Office of the Chief of Military History, U.S. Army. (1969). *United States Army in World War II: Mediterranean Theater of Operations – Salerno to Cassino.* Washington D.C.:
Parker, P. (2009). *The Last Veteran: Harry Patch and the Legacy of War.* London: Fourth Estate.
Pilpel, R.H. (1976). *Churchill in America, 1895–1961: an affectionate portrait.* New York: Harcourt Brace.
Prefer, N.N. (2019). Lucian K. Truscott: The Soldier's General. *Warfare History Network.*
Rennie, K.R. (2021). *The Destruction and Recovery of Monte Cassino.* Amsterdam: Amsterdam University Press.
Renwick, R. (1996). *Fighting With Allies.* London: Macmillan.
Reynolds, D.D. (1988). *An Ocean Apart.* New York: Random House.
Richardson, D.H. (1984). *Monte Cassino.* New York: Cingdon & Weed Inc.
Robinson, F. (19 October 1889). Convict Life at Wormwood Scrubs. *The Graphic.*
Roosevelt, F. (1943). *Casablanca Conference Radio address, 12 February 1943.* Washington DC: The Public Papers of F.D. Roosevelt, Vol. 12, p. 71.
Roosevelt, F.D. (1944). *The Wisdom of FDR.* New York: Carrol Publishing Group.
Scoular, C. (2015). *Irish History for the Inquisitive: stories of intrigue, hope, farce and devastating loss.* Killyleagh, County Down: Clive Scoular.
Smith, E.D. (1975). *The Battles for Cassino.* New York: Charles Scribner's Sons.
St Louis Post-Dispatch. (24 July 1943). American troops occupy Marsala, p.1.
Stelzer, C. (2012). *Dinner with Churchill: policy-making at the dinner table.* London: Short.
Sunderland Daily Echo and Shipping Gazette. (3 September 1939). Mr Churchill Speaks.
The Pictorial History of the 36th Infantry 'Texas' Division. (1946). Houston: 36th Infantry Division Association.
Trevelyan, R. (1981). *Rome '44.* London: Secker & Warburg.
Trumbull, H. (1968). *Soft underbelly: the Anglo-American controversy over the Italian campaign, 1939–1945.* New York: Macmillan.
US News and World Report. (1945). *Biennial Report of the Chief of Staff of the US Army.* New York.
Vere, D.I. (2006). *Give us this Day.* Milton Keynes: AuthorHouse.
Walker, F.L. (1969). *From Texas to Rome.* Dallas: Taylor Publishing Company.

Wallace, R. (1987). *The Italian Campaign.* Alexandria, VA: Time-Life Books.

Webb, R.N. (1969). *Winston Churchill – Man of the Century.* New York: Franklin Watts.

Whicker, A. (2006). *Whicker's War.* London: Harper Collins.

Whiting, C. (1992). *Slaughter over Sicily.* Barnsley: Pen & Sword.

Wilson, C. (1966). *Churchill Taken from the Diaries of Lord Moran.* Boston: Houghton Mifflin

Wrigley, C. (2006). *Churchill.* London: Haus.

INDEX